THE ART AND MAKING OF

HANNIBAL

THE TELEVISION SERIES

THANK YOU

Titan Books would like to thank all the members of the cast and crew of *Hannibal* who gave up their time, supplied materials, and were amazingly generous and excited for this book to take shape. A special thank you must go to Bryan Fuller for creating such a stylized and beautiful show and for contributing his time and enthusiasm to this project. Huge thanks also to the people at NBC Universal, Gaumont and Evolution, who helped make this book happen. Extra thanks go to Kirsti Tichenor at Evolution and *Hannibal* producer Loretta Ramos whose unwavering dedication and love for the show shines through on every page.

THE ART & MAKING OF HANNIBAL: THE TELEVISION SERIES
ISBN: 9781783295753

Published by Titan Books
A division of Titan Publishing Group Ltd.
144 Southwark St.
London
SE1 0UP

First edition: April 2015
10 9 8 7 6 5 4 3 2 1

To receive advance information, news, competitions, and exclusive offers online, please sign up for the Titan newsletter on our website: www.titanbooks.com

Did you enjoy this book? We love to hear from our readers. Please e-mail us at: readerfeedback@titanemail.com or write to Reader Feedback at the above address.

A CIP catalogue record for this title is available from the British Library.

Printed and bound in the USA.

THE ART AND MAKING OF

HANNIBAL

THE TELEVISION SERIES

JESSE MCLEAN

TITANBOOKS

CONTENTS

APÉRITIF

FOREWORD
BY MARTHA DE LAURENTIIS

I t's hard for me to believe it has been more than 30 years since my husband Dino and I first read Thomas Harris' novel *Red Dragon* and felt it would make a fantastic film. Most books that inspire film and television contain some kernel of brilliance you love, but you're usually conscious that an adaptation will have to drastically reimagine major aspects of what's on the page. From the beginning, however, it was clear that in *Red Dragon*, it was all already there.

Especially, it created its own original world out of fairly familiar thriller terrain, one which was simultaneously both fascinating and terrifying. A world in which working-class FBI agents utilized Sherlock Holmes-clever deduction and cutting-edge science and technology pursuing killers who were compelled by some deeply personal, insanely twisted grandiosity. Thomas Harris had worked as a journalist, and he had done extensive research into

both serial killers and profiling techniques that were at the time unfamiliar to the general public. You felt that research and authority in his writing.

But there was so much more than the verisimilitude and clever plotting one expects from a great procedural thriller. The characters were archetypal, but layered, unusually strong but surprisingly vulnerable. There was a romance to the way these solitary characters obsessively went about their work. The infernally complicated relationship between Hannibal and Will leapt off the page. Description focused on moody, Gothic details that made you see our world a little more interestingly. So long as you weren't the one ending up on the autopsy table, you wanted to spend more time in the world of Will Graham and Hannibal Lecter, in the imagination of Thomas Harris.

Like all of Thomas Harris' fans, I eagerly awaited each new book, through their many-year-long periods of research, gestation and writing, waiting to see where he'd take the characters next. When it became clear that Thomas had finished the *Hannibal* saga, I felt a bit of sadness, as a reader even more than a producer involved with the films. Suspecting that I wasn't the only one who wanted to spend more time in this world, I started to think about its potential for television. So much of what makes *Hannibal* itself would have been unimaginable on network television even a decade ago, but with the recent renaissance in television, a lot of the rules have fallen away or evolved, offering great potential for serialized storytelling.

When I first discussed the possibility of a *Hannibal* television show with Thomas, he asked a profoundly challenging question. "Who could possibly write it?" And he followed that with a daunting admonition, "Just don't screw it up!" Actually, I think the wording was a bit less polite than that.

 I count myself incredibly fortunate that my producing partners at Gaumont International TV set a meeting with Bryan Fuller to pitch us his take on the show. Before the meeting, Bryan didn't strike me as the most obvious match; I knew him for quirky, soulful, original shows with a dark comic edge. However, Bryan proved to be the biggest *Hannibal* and Thomas Harris fan I had ever met. He had an encyclopedic memory of all the books. He had a brilliant, fully-realized approach into utilizing the books and freshly telling their story. But mainly, he loved the books as much as I do, and he was passionate about doing something that respected what Thomas had created.

Bryan has of course expanded and reinterpreted the Hannibal universe. The Will Graham of *Red Dragon* is somewhat different, in both personality and job description, than in our *Hannibal* series. The Wendigo representing Will's own dark side, and his method of mentally reconstructing crime scenes, are both more Bryan Fuller than Thomas Harris. Yet, while I'm continually blown away by the imaginations and crafts of Bryan and the other writers, I still feel like there's something about these pieces of original invention that's true to the DNA of Thomas' work. Even when something is fantastical, the emotional truth is more powerful than the shock value.

When NBC read Bryan's pilot, they immediately ordered a full season of 13 episodes. It was a coup. Of course, as the series became closer to reality, people began to ask, "But who could possibly play Hannibal after Anthony Hopkins?"

As you know, we've found a fantastic cast. Seeing the show, no one asks how Mads Mikkelsen could follow Sir Anthony. He has captured his own impossible combination of charm, genius, and evil that exists separate but alongside Anthony Hopkins' immortal, Oscar-winning performance. Hugh Dancy has found depths to Will Graham so we never ask how someone so brilliant can be so tortured. Casting Laurence Fishburne as Jack Crawford brought a gravitas that made the FBI chief a more pivotal role. All the recurring cast members have added new life and dimension to the world of *Hannibal*, and we've attracted wonderful actors even for one-off roles as killers and victims.

With this book, you'll be able to step behind the curtain and see many of the people actively involved in recreating and expanding this world at work: the artists, builders, cast members, cinematographers, directors, writers, and production staff. For a filmmaker, revealing the magic is always fraught with anxiety. It's the impression in the viewer's head that you want to be really memorable. What you don't fully grasp can be richer and more terrifying than what is seen. But looking through the book, I think you'll sense that as terrific as the costuming, make-up or murdered-corpse-building may be, none of it is empty style-for-style's sake. It's in service of characters and ideas that are human and provocative, a universe of its own that's too real and emotional to be easily demystified, and one that we all want to continue to explore.

I hope you enjoy it.

Martha De Laurentiis

ENTRÉE

HANNIBAL MEETS BRYAN FULLER

Fans of the novels by Thomas Harris are well-acquainted with the idea of "becoming". Fans of *Hannibal* are likely familiar with the theme as well. They are also aware of it in the very creation of the show and the manner in which the show creator seeks to "transform" the existing Thomas Harris canon into a universe that is at once recognizable but also unlike anything we've seen.

Ostensibly adapted from *Red Dragon*, the first novel to introduce Hannibal Lecter to the world, Bryan Fuller's *Hannibal* is an in-depth investigation into what is referred to in passing in the novel—that Graham consulted with Lecter on the profiling of a serial killer before realizing that the good doctor was a killer wolf in tweed clothing.

That the genesis of such a relationship would make for good TV viewing is understandable, but one can imagine the daunting task of approaching such a well-known literary property in a manner that would satisfy both the Thomas Harris faithful and the viewing public at large.

But how did a man previously known for smart, whimsical shows about reluctant grim reapers and pie-makers with the powers of raising the dead wind up making one of the most gripping, terrifying shows on television?

Like many things, the story behind how Bryan Fuller became involved with adapting Thomas Harris to televsion has a lot to do with chance. And the siren call of Broadway.

After completing work on a script, Fuller needed a trip to New York to recharge. While on a Gotham-bound flight to take in a few palette-cleansing shows, he found himself sitting behind his old friend Katie O'Connell. After catching up, she revealed that as the CEO of the new U.S. TV arm of the legendary Gaumont Film Company (the oldest and longest continuously operating studio, founded in 1895), her next order of business was the development of a television series around the most famous fictional psychiatrist in all literature.

When asked if he thought this was viable as a series, Fuller was quick to say yes. It wasn't until after the flight was over, however, that he was able to articulate his approach.

"There was much in the literature that was not explored in the films," Fuller says. "So it really felt like it was ripe for the reinterpretation."

A fan of the novels since high school, Fuller appreciated the hallmarks of the author's style and how it would work in a serialized format.

"It feels like such a signature of Thomas Harris' work," Fuller says of the novel *Red Dragon*. "To blend together genres so seamlessly where you're not quite sure if you're watching a horror movie or a crime thriller."

Not only was the idea to approach it as a prequel to previous incarnations, but an intriguing "DJ mash-up" style that not only reinvented the universe of the novels but also fit neatly in with the "Harrisian" theme of transformation.

"We take tracks from the novel *Hannibal* and are spinning them with lyrics from the novel *Red Dragon*.

"We started robbing from the future to pay the present," Fuller notes, arguing that the approach resulted in thinking "Ooh! That's a great nugget, let's use it now instead of waiting to use it when it is more temporally sound and linked to the literature."

This approach is essential to attracting and keeping Thomas Harris fans.

"I guess it would have been possible to just sit down with the first novel and make a thirteen hour

TV show," actor Hugh Dancy says. "There's certainly enough there. But, at the same time, too many people know that story too well."

The remix angle was taken to Martha De Laurentiis, an executive producer of the series and head of the equally legendary De Laurentiis Company, who also had a stake in the Hannibal Lecter legacy.

"They came right away to see me and it was indeed what perfectly fit...the period right before *Red Dragon* and using the mythology of Thomas Harris' writing which is what sold me on it," De Laurentiis says. "Bryan wanted to make something he would want to see. I know Bryan's taste is impeccable, and he's a very classy writer and if it was something that he would want to see, I knew that I could trust Bryan to deliver something intriguing and different."

Certainly, *Hannibal* stands alone in the television landscape, notable not only for the high calibre of performances and the finely-tuned aesthetic vision but for the sheer quantity of blood and gore.

In conversations with Jennifer Salke at NBC Entertainment about the kind of show they were doing, Fuller said, "This is a horror show. This is about a cannibal psychiatrist, and one of pop culture's most iconic villains." To do anything but give service to the horror elements of the story risked alienating the core audience of such a show, be they fans of horror in general or Hannibal in particular. An earlier take on the show would have kept Hannibal as a peripheral figure, an idea that Martha De Laurentiis rightly notes was way off base. "You don't use up a character like Hannibal, who's going to eat up the screen, in the background."

Salke agreed and vowed to allow Fuller to produce the show he envisioned.

"And she kept her promise," says Fuller.

That said, there are limits to what can be shown on a network show as dictated by the network's Broadcast Standards and Practices department. This arm of the broadcaster is responsible for monitoring the content of shows aired with a particular eye on violence and sexuality. One could easily think that the relationship

between this department and the team making *Hannibal* might be contentious.

Instead, Fuller and his team have forged a more collaborative arrangement. Whenever there is a scene that promises to test the boundaries (and even the strongest stomach), Fuller initiates a conversation in advance.

"I reach out and say, 'This is something from the book that we would like to do. It's fairly graphic...can you help us navigate so we can show as much as we possibly can?'"

As it turns out, it *is* possible, provided certain rules are followed.

"The redder the blood and the brighter the blood the less you can show," Fuller elaborates. "So if you darken the blood and throw it into shadow, then you can be much more graphic than you normally would be able to."

The elegant, if bloody, mayhem inspires a great deal of respect for the man in charge of the show, whose guiding hand is felt at every level of production.

About that attention to the detail and the big picture, Mads Mikkelsen is unequivocal.

"His universe, his brain, is working on a different level than anybody else I've ever met. It does not only go with the creative process of creating the characters, it's down to the smallest detail with the costumes, the casting, how the hair should be on an extra. He's very visual and for that reason he cannot keep his hands away from anything on this production and it's quite fantastic."

Not only are people happy to work with a visionary like Bryan Fuller, they are also drawn to the creative freedom that work on a show like *Hannibal* presents.

François Dagenais of Mindwarp FX, the prosthetics wizard behind many of the most shocking moments in the series, finds that the unique challenges paired with punishing television deadlines are premium-grade fuel.

"'Build a horse. Let's put somebody in it. Let's have a bird flying out!' I like to create."

Christopher Hargadon, the costume designer on the

show responsible for Hannibal's bespoke plaid suits as well as every other character's wardrobe, says that he has been waiting his entire career to work with a person of Fuller's refined and definitive tastes.

"The thing that's very enjoyable and easy about Bryan is that he's not wishy-washy," Hargadon says. "He has immediate reactions to things and he never goes back on them. He doesn't vacillate. I have had that good fortune previously, but he is at the limit of it."

Anthony Patterson of Rocket Science VFX (the effects house responsible for the arresting CG effects of the stag, and the Wendigo), also mentions Fuller's full-throttle eighteen-hour day dedication to the show, much of that time spent refining script pages.

As showrunner, no scene is blocked without Fuller's complete approval at the script stage. The call sheets for the next day's shooting are issued by the assistant directors, who write the initials 'BF' beside scene numbers that Fuller has approved.

"There would be several empty ones," Patterson says.

"So the next day we'd arrive on set and there would be a new set of pages for those scenes that Bryan had written overnight, that the actors had to adapt and we had to adapt to for visual effects."

Or as Production Designer Matthew Davies puts it, "Bryan grooms every script, polishes every line of dialogue, and I think that is true of the design."

Davies notes that Fuller is just as exacting when it comes to the dressing of each set, all in service of the unique gothic hybrid of a show that he described from the onset as 'a very elegant horror film'. As evidence, Davies points to a $45,000 piece required for a recovery room in the show's second season.

"He wanted a George Nakashima bench [and] they're not readily available," Davies says. "His genius is that he will ask for something that might seem beyond the realm of possibility but it is often those grand gestures that inform the spirit of the show and give it its rich aesthetic of Hannibal's rich cultural appreciation."

Fuller's desire to transform the world of Thomas Harris into a unique experience does not stop at just

[Below] Bryan Fuller (left) and cinematographer James Hawkinson (right) on set for the first episode of season one.

the creation of the television series, although he is quick to pay tribute to the power of that theme in the existing novels.

"I feel that the theme of transformation is very Harrisian at its core," Fuller says, "because if you look at all of the villains in Thomas Harris' work...these are all men who are on some arc of transformation, whether it is physical transformation, psychological transformation or just the fire of revenge burning off any last semblance of your humanity so you can be a higher power. That is just part of how Thomas Harris writes his villains, so we very much wanted to make sure that we were telling a transformation story, and continue to tell a transformation story. I think that

is what is at the root of, at least my fascination with, psychology is not just about how it works but how it can change."

In fact, Fuller hopes to alter how people see Hannibal Lecter and the universe that whirls around him.

"I would love for this to be the definitive Hannibal Lecter story."

Given the iconic performances already offered in Hannibal's name, this is no meek aspiration. And Fuller's Hannibal wouldn't want it any other way.

"I would be a little disappointed if he wasn't trying to," Mikkelsen says. "Meaning that he has a chance that you do not have doing films. He's got hour after hour to explore it and dig into this character and into this universe. So obviously our goal is to give a portrait of a man that is as elaborate as we can do in this medium."

DAVID SLADE

It isn't surprising to hear David Slade refer to his approach to making *Hannibal* in cinematic terms, especially when relating his Thousand Post-It Notes theory of filmmaking.

"At a certain point of complexity you can't hold the film in your head so you start putting down Post-It notes and you very quickly get to a thousand."

Considering the bountiful literary, artistic and cinematic references peppered throughout the series, you can't help but wonder if one thousand Post-Its are enough.

The responsibility of directing the pilot episode of a series is immense. Not only is there an inordinate amount of level-setting for the dramatic universe of the show, the visual language of that episode has to be rich and accessible enough to see an audience through many chapters.

And choosing that director is no easy task either, especially for a show that has such a distinct aesthetic style matched with a Giallo-style flair for bloody mayhem. It is easy to see how the man behind the punishing psychological thrills of *Hard Candy* and the existential vampiric terrors of *30 Days of Night* would seem like the logical choice.

Also, it doesn't hurt to live in the same neighbourhood as the creator of the show, especially if you are involved in the development of the series at an early stage.

"Really early. The first script was finished six months before we shot it," Slade says. "It turns out that Bryan and I live quite close to each other and there is a coffee shop very local to both of us. We met there... and at that point they had Hugh Dancy and Bryan said to me, 'What do you think of Mads Mikkelsen?' And I said, 'Oh my God...he'd be amazing.'"

Other than having input on the casting of principals, Slade also had the luck of working with a writer like Bryan Fuller, who possesses not only a broad vision for the show but a manner of writing that appeals to a visually-inclined filmmaker. Often, TV writing can become bogged down in exposition-heavy scenes loaded with blocks of dialogue, but the pilot script for *Hannibal* was something quite different.

"Bryan has a very visual way of thinking and I value

that because God knows it's hard enough to do a really, really good job but if somebody actually writes down words that equate to great images, it's a great start."

Preparation for shooting the pilot "Apéritif" was sure to include a great deal of thinking and deciding on the visual tone of the show, but did present Slade with a great opportunity for research.

"My homework was to read this great literature," he says of Harris' novels. "And to have fun with it. And to figure out if there's an image to take to Bryan... 'There's this image on page forty-seven. It's a great metaphor for what we're doing.'"

Other reading included *Hunting Humans: The Rise of the Modern Multiple Murderer* by Elliott Leyton, a Canadian social-anthropologist and world-renowned consultant on the topic of serial murder. Among the pages that detailed the grisly methods of horrific killers, Slade found an intensely moral book and one that informed how he thought violence should be handled on the show.

"Every page is telling you how horrible these people are and how this can never be about celebrating the crazy things that they do. So when it gets to a point where someone gives you a note saying, 'Well, it would be better if we didn't see the blood,' you think, 'Of

course, we have to see the blood.' That's part of the process...it's horrible and you have to feel it."

As Slade points out, the standard handling of violence on television is antiseptic and without much in the way of consequence ("You fire a gun and people fall on the ground and that's it, we go off to the next scene"). While steeped in gruesome effects, *Hannibal* is very much about the cost of violence, seen most clearly in the arc of Will Graham's character. From his (necessary) murder of Garret Jacob Hobbs to the toll of his empathy with serial killers, Graham suffers incredibly from vicious acts.

"It's a show about the horror and the danger of looking at violence in detail," Slade says. "And having to look at it over and over again and what that does to a character."

Slade found that his approach with the two lead actors was as different as the characters they were playing. For Hugh Dancy's portrayal of Will Graham, he took a gently interrogative angle.

"My process with Hugh at the very beginning of the first episode was to ask him questions, over and over, asking him questions to answer as Will...to get to a point where we had consistency."

They also spent time honing in on the physical inhabitation of Graham.

As well as a filmmaker, David Slade (far right), is an accomplished photographer. All images on these four pages, save the one of himself, were taken by Slade during production.

"A lot of it was rooted in his anxiety and his tension and figuring out where and when to drop or increase that."

The approach with Mads Mikkelsen took a more theoretical bent.

"With Mads, it's incredibly conceptual," Slade reports. "[Hannibal] is the Devil, he is omniscient, he is the smartest person in the room. And if you start from that position, the character falls beautifully together...Mads is going to become the defining face of this character."

Likely it didn't take one thousand Post-It Notes for David Slade to arrive at that conclusion.

MAIN
COURSE

HANNIBAL

MADS MIKKELSEN

To contemplate joining a network television show such as *Hannibal* must have included many questions, including whether or not you are prepared for the grueling hours, the extreme conditions of location work and, in this case, why take on a character as iconic as Dr. Lecter?

"It was quite intimidating joining this boat," Mikkelsen says. "Obviously there are a couple of guys who have done it to perfection before me."

A deciding factor was the terrain Bryan Fuller and his

"Obviously he is an intelligent man, he understands what he is doing," Mikkelsen reasons. "It's not that he wakes up one morning and goes, 'Oh my God, what have I done?'"

However, the nature of evil and those who perpetrate it is never far from his mind.

"He talks about evilness a lot. He talks about God but he doesn't see God as evil and he also has all these examples...making a church roof collapse on praying people. That's the irony of God. We don't call Him evil,

CLOTHES & STYLE

The approach Mads Mikkelsen takes in playing Hannibal Lecter, while not exclusively rooted in his clothing, is certainly helped by a sort of haberdashery method.

"I am always wearing Adidas runners, track and sports clothing," he says. "I am from that generation that is always ready to play some ball. So for me to step into his three-piece suits is always a giant change and it kind of kick-starts you for the morning."

Costume designer Christopher Hargadon knew that bold yet sophisticated choices would best suit a man like Lecter.

"I understood what his character was like," he says. "That he would be refined, have money, that he would have taste."

Hargadon put together a few different combinations to build Hannibal's closet and presented them to Fuller for review, who had a very strong response to the fabrics of checks and plaids.

"That was a resource I depleted quite quickly," Hargadon says. "But then I started to find in Europe suppliers who do beautiful blends of Scottish wool."

Once the fabric was selected, the main concern was finding Lecter's silhouette. Hargadon strove for a strong profile that had a pronounced fashion-forward edge but with a slight period feel, an amalgam that respected Lecter's creative flair but also held a respect for the past he carries with him.

There is always a concern when a concept morphs from drawing board to reality—what makes sense for a character may not compliment the actor playing the part. This was not an issue with Mikkelsen.

"Mads is an athlete and a dancer and a gymnast," Hargadon says. "I think you could put anything on the guy and it would work."

There is still the issue of conflicting priorities—like Hannibal's home, what works thematically versus believability. "Our eye has been trained over time to leave the norm and banality," Hargadon notes. "To have a little bit of excitement in the clothing...and now I think there's a certain amount of leeway in the world of reality."

For example, he wouldn't put Jack Crawford's boss Kade Prurnell (played by Cynthia Nixon) into a strapless cocktail dress.

"But I would put her in an Escada, form-fitting dress...I try to make people a little outside of the box but still make sense with the story."

As for the man who wears the suits on set, Mikkelsen sees his wardrobe on *Hannibal* as a first.

"It's probably the first show or film I've been on where there is a single male actor who has the biggest budget on costumes. But Hannibal is quite elaborate in his tastes, so the budget is up there."

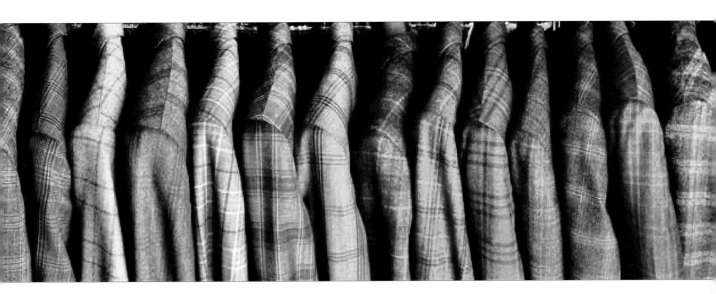

HANNIBAL'S OFFICE

Aaron Morrison, in the show's art department, created the sketches which litter Hannibal's office.

Patti Podesta, the production designer for the very first episode and consultant on the first two episodes of season two, cites the essay "Coldness and Cruelty" by Gilles Deleuze on the nature of masochism and sadism when discussing what initially drew her to the project. Known for her elegant work in both film (*Memento, Smart People, Love & Other Drugs*) and television (*Awake, Homeland, Elementary*), Podesta recalled reading the piece in university and how well it fit Fuller's take on the legendary psychiatrist.

"The sadist needs to obliterate an object that has become a sign for the world or nature, in order to commune with his own reconstructed nature," she says. "This was one of the reasons I took it on, because Hannibal is producing his own re-natured nature... and that everything around him would be produced with this idea of the obliteration of actual nature to have a sort of perfection."

Part of that perfection, the face that Hannibal presents to the world, is in his surroundings. With that in mind, Podesta and Fuller spoke at length about how a man such as Lecter would smuggle himself into the modern world undetected.

"One of the things we were talking about was how Hannibal 'passes' in polite society," Podesta recalls. They wanted to show him as a man of incredible sophistication and education, as well as one with an acute sense of style.

"We thought about using a historical building that he might have taken over," Podesta says. "That would give us a reason for having something more elaborate than your typical psychiatrist's office, which we know are really a series of rat mazes."

Concurrent with the search for fantastical inspiration was an urge to also keep the office rooted in reality. Podesta was familiar with the city of Baltimore and endeavoured to create such a space that would be found in that atmosphere.

[Left] Jack and Hannibal at their first meeting in season one, episode one. The sketches become an integral part of the story and seal Miriam Lass' fate.

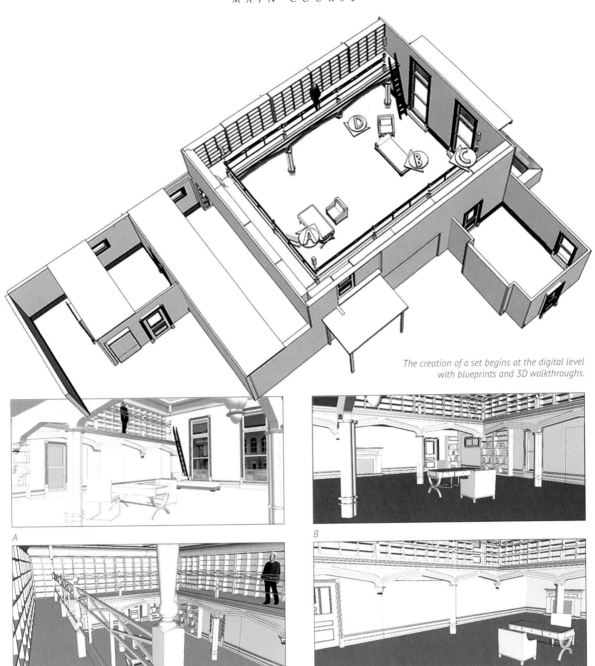

The creation of a set begins at the digital level with blueprints and 3D walkthroughs.

A

B

C

D

"I found this picture of the North Carolina State Library in a design book about historical buildings," Podesta says of the space designed by Scottish-born David Paton, who apprenticed in England with the highly-respected neoclassicist Sir John Soane.

"[The library] had those arches," Podesta says. "It had those catwalks overhead and those beautiful columns. Bryan looked at it and said, 'That's it!'"

From there, it was a matter of adorning the room to fit Hannibal's taste, combining an art

"Don't psychoanalyse me. You wouldn't like me when I'm psychoanalysed." *Will Graham.*

nouveau influence by way of his European background and the severity of modern Danish furniture.

"We always conceived it as being a mix of things that would really be an encyclopedia about him...as much as he would want it to be."

The influence of Sir John Soane went beyond his design style (even if his library was cited specifically in Fuller's pilot script).

"He was one of the first people to make a collection of historical objects and paintings in a cabinet his own encyclopedic vision in his office," Podesta says. "We're starting our Hannibal with that backstory, that he lived in Florence prior to opening up his psychiatry practice in the United States."

Matthew Davies, the production designer who took over from Podesta after the first episode of season one,

makes a point about the colour scheme of the office which neatly dramatizes the slash of violence beneath the elegant veneer.

"It's very much a grey-based palette. However there are points of quite intense colour: the colour red that appears in Hannibal's office, one entire wall is red, the red stripes in the curtains."

But what place does casting have, if any, in the art of production design? Certainly this will vary from film to TV, and project to project, but Podesta confirms that what actor is inhabiting each character will have an impact on the creation of a space.

"But more often than not the cast is not in place during the key pre-production period in which we conceptualize the universe of the show," she says. "And this was the case with the casting of Mads."

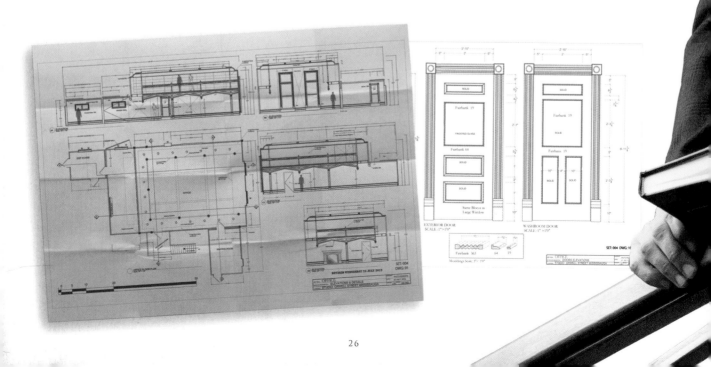

Podesta was pleased at the prospect of having as graceful an actor as Mads Mikkelsen take on the nefarious Dr. Hannibal Lecter.

"We were already building the office when he came to the project," Podesta reports. "But I must say that when I was told he would be playing Lecter I was so very excited.

And from the first day on set, his characterization eclipsed all my hopes...the way he moves his body and his screen presence; he's a phenomena! And that phenomena certainly occupied my psyche as I conceived the other sets I designed for the series."

As for the inspiration other iterations of the Thomas

Harris universe provided, Podesta went back to the source material.

"I read *Hannibal* when David Slade first mentioned the project to me and it set me to thinking about the nature of sadism," Podesta recalls. "I had seen *Silence of the Lambs* of course...and I caught it again on TV in the early stages of conceptualizing the project. It seemed a cleaned up version of the mind and activities of the sadist as described in *Hannibal*. Which was, really, the concept that intrigued me, in a philosophical way, about taking on the material."

[Bottom Right] Detailed architectural floorplan of Hannibal's balcony, right down to the exact width of the moulding on the columns.

THE FOOD

In the introduction to his essay, "Coldness and Cruelty", Gilles Deleuze makes an interesting point regarding the naming of diseases.

"Illnesses are sometimes named after typical patients, but more often it is the doctor's name that is given to the disease—Roger's disease, Parkinson's disease, etc."

That begs the question: Is Hannibal Lecter, in his extra-curricular culinary pursuits, creating just such a clinical picture? If so, then perhaps we can apply that to Lecter's appetites. If 'cannibalism' is the act of a human eating another human's flesh, then perhaps we can say that 'Hannibalism' is when one person eats another for committing the perceived sin of rudeness.

If so, then such a man's kitchen must be equally up to the task. And if his office is elaborate and faceted, then Hannibal's kitchen is economical and severe.

"His movements are precise...choreographed," Podesta says. "He wants to be able to look at the meats and the dishes like tableaus as he creates them.

"We also wanted the set to have a bit of the flavour of a laboratory or morgue."

In keeping with the cold yet serene funereal feel, Matthew Davies points out the importance of the colour scheme in the kitchen.

"The greys in Hannibal's kitchen are not truly grey, they're not black and white, there are hues of purple in there and hues of the cobalt walls from the dining

room. There's a very subtle colour language going on in the kitchen."

Which raises the question: How does a designer weigh the pragmatic aspects of creating a space along with the thematic concerns of the story? Does a kitchen that reflects the artistic vision of a character also need to look like a functioning room?

It depends.

"I think the degree of pragmatism changes from set to set," Podesta says. "I've done quite a bit of residential design and know the specs for high-end kitchens, and this was in my mind laying out Lecter's because there is a flow to kitchen workspaces and appliances that enables the right choreography."

But it also had to serve as a dramatic space, as a place of performance for Lecter before he presents his creations to unwitting guests. As a result, there is

an unmistakable familiarity to Lecter's kitchen that is difficult to pinpoint until Podesta removes all doubt.

"It resembles a cooking show set."

In the dark auditorium that is Hannibal Lecter's house, however, the kitchen could be seen as the shadowy wings for his final performance space.

"If his kitchen is his backstage," Podesta says. "Then his dining room is like the completely dressed, opulent theatre."

Even when he eats alone, Hannibal is aware of the theatricality of his dining room; the white molding across the top of the room frames his table like a proscenium arch.

The design of the room also harkens back to Podesta's view of the sadist and his own "re-natured nature".

"He is in this voluptuous, artificial environment and

[Below] Original sketches from food stylist Janice Poon detailing a fig and foie gras platter used in season one, episode four, "Coquilles".

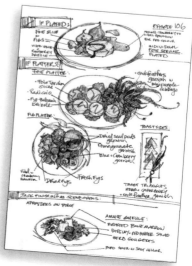

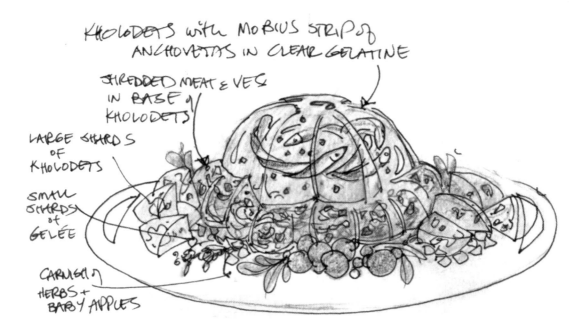

KHOLODETS with MOBIUS STRIP of
ANCHOVETTES IN CLEAR GELATINE

SHREDDED MEAT & VEG
IN BASE of
KHOLODETS

LARGE SHARDS
OF
KHOLODETS

SMALL
SHARDS
of
GELÉE

CARNISON
HERBS +
BABY APPLES

completely self-conscious of his own position in it and his own pleasure of it."

Even a diabolical genius like Lecter cannot control nature, but he can certainly recreate it to serve his own needs. A great example of this is the tamed flora of the herb wall which is anchored by a wallpaper reproduction of a nature etching by Oscar Grosch.

Another are the sturdy yet curvilinear blue walls, achieved by stacked mouldings which are reminiscent of the dark night sky.

"When it came to the blue walls in the dining room that was entirely Bryan," Matthew Davies notes. "He had his own reference point to that, that deep cobalt colour."

The accents throughout the house offer a palette that is almost as exceptional on a television series as the erudite and elegant tone of the scripts.

"I think the balance of working with very exotic and interesting finishes and rich textures and then combining them with those dual-tone accents creates a much more evolved aesthetic that is rare in television," Davies says.

In keeping with Hannibal's desire to exert control over nature, floral arrangements are also a big component on the show.

"We spend thousands of dollars every episode creating elaborate floral displays that are all pre-approved by Bryan," Davies says. "Every dinner party has themed florals."

When the odious Frederick Chilton was invited to Lecter's for dinner, the arrangements were fashioned to reflect the recently-eviscerated doctor's new-found vegetarianism (after all, it's tough to digest protein-rich foods when you're missing a few organs).

"The entire floral arrangement is made of fruits and vegetables."

For other engagements, the florals were made of animal products.

CAVIAR PLATTER

STAR GAZY PIE

SHELLS OF TRI COLOUR CAVIAR ON ICE
SALMON, GOLDEN & BLACK
with
MINI BLINIS

STURGEON HEAD PIE from
GOGOL'S "DEAD SOULS"
(ZAKUSKI DINNER of POLICE CHIEF)

Further sketches from Janice Poon [left] and the finished products [below]

"There's a couple of pyramid-like structures that sit on top of the sideboard and the trolley," Davies says. "They were made up of bird's feathers and skulls and beetles and butterflies...this rich menagerie of animals."

The animal imagery continues into his living room. Show creator Bryan Fuller shares Hannibal Lecter's rarefied aesthetic sensibilities. All the better for the production team when scripts for the show call for unusually specific furnishings.

"Bryan loves horse imagery," Davies says. Hannibal's living room chairs were obtained from Fuller's own shop. "They have carved horse's hooves for feet."

If Fuller shares an aesthetic kinship with Lecter, then world-famous chef and *Hannibal* culinary consultant, José Andrés, enjoys a gastronomical affinity with him— that is, in spirit if not in actual ingredients.

"I've always felt a connection to Hannibal," Andrés says. "I really believe that there is something innate in our human DNA that attracts us to blood. To be able to examine that desire through Hannibal's mind is fascinating. He's such an intriguing and complex character, and his big, theatrical performances have always resonated with me."

Born in Spain, Andrés is often cited as the man responsible for bringing tapas dining to America. Outside of teaching a culinary physics course at Harvard, he also has restaurants in Washington D.C., Beverly Hills, Las Vegas, Miami Beach, Bethesda, Arlington, and the Puerto Rican town of Dorado. As to how he became involved with *Hannibal*, it has as much to do with location as his impeccable cookery skills.

"When you're running a restaurant in Los Angeles, you never know who's going to walk through the door. One night, Bryan Fuller came in and told me about his project. I didn't hesitate to jump at the chance to work with him."

For Andrés, the notion that Hannibal equals cannibalism alone is short-sighted.

"It's so much deeper than that. It's a look into human evolution; it's about getting inside the brain

A

B

C

[Above & right] 3D rendered layouts of Hannibal's home, including kitchen and dining area as well as a garden which is rarely seen on screen. Below, Mads Mikkelsen and the crew shooting a scene in the season two premiere.

of a person and figuring out how food is going to help us understand who that person is. He's a Renaissance man but he also embraces science and technology."

Creating dishes that allow us a window into the brain of Hannibal Lecter is very much a collaborative process, and one that begins in the script phase.

"Sometimes, Bryan will email me in the middle of the night, at like 4am, and say 'José, what are some things that make us as humans tastier?'"

While a message like that would result in a call to the police for most people, it is standard procedure on

[Above] An interior sketch by Patti Podesta laying out Hannibal's dining room and the final set [left].

Hannibal. And yet it is bracing all the same.

"I could be sleeping in bed or walking the streets of Tokyo, but I'm always ready to jump in," Andrés says. "Imagine how unique it is to receive an email with a script, this living thing that's changing and evolving right before your eyes."

The initial collaboration will often start while Fuller is still in the writer's room, and both Andrés and food stylist Janice Poon are on the receiving end of those eerie late-night messages. All three engage in conversations that can take many emails, and last anywhere from several hours, to a few days, to even a few weeks, all in an effort to bring a dish to life and make it perfect.

"We all share roles and positions throughout the process," Andrés says. "The only thing that varies is the episode itself. Each dish is based on what's going on in that episode, so our process is always different."

Janice Poon echoes the sentiment, especially in her praise of Fuller's end of the process. "I can't talk about his genius enough," she says. "He's that kind of genius where it's surprising every time. You think you've heard of everything and then he comes up with an idea... And he does it every bloody time."

That's not to say that her work is without trials or last-minute changes to the script.

In "Futamono" (season two, episode six), the story as written called for Hannibal to enjoy a dish of lasagna with Alana Bloom. An email after midnight the day before shooting was hauntingly titled: "Hi Everyone! We would like to do a braised roast of Eddie Izzard's thigh."

Andrés suggested that the roast should be cooked in clay so that it might better resonate with Biblical gravitas ("Whereas you saw the feet and toes, partly of potter's clay and partly of iron, the kingdom shall be divided." Daniel 2:41).

Once Poon made the decision on how to best replicate a human thigh (two double pork loins invisibly sewn together), there was the matter of creating enough of them for repeated takes and preparing them in the clay so they were camera-ready.

"It was crazy-making," Poon says. "After a while, the meat will dry out. And the director wanted to show breaking [the mold] and the first cut and they wanted to do it all in one continuous shot."

Poon set about creating eight roasts but one burst in the oven, so seven were delivered to the set. Everyone agreed that the meat should ooze juice on the first cut, which would not present a problem with a standard roast. Poon knew from her years as a food stylist in

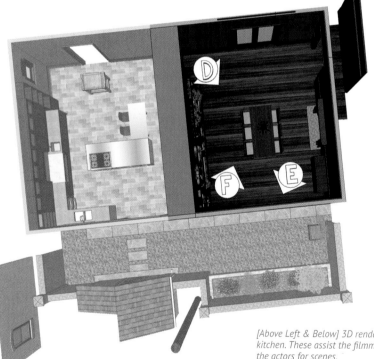

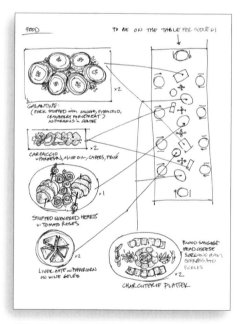

[Above Left & Below] 3D rendered floorplans and virtual walkthroughs of Hannibal's kitchen. These assist the filmmakers when it comes to setting up shots and positioning the actors for scenes.
[Above Right] A sketch from Janice Poon detailing the banquet produced for season one, episode seven, "Sorbet".

D

E

F

television, film and advertising, that a simple injection with a water-filled hypodermic would produce the required result.

"You try injecting a roast wrapped in clay," Poon says. "That's not in the manual."

Because the director wanted the first cut of the roast to follow the cracking of the clay mold, and all done in one take, the needle had to be coaxed through the clay shell.

"It's not in the manual the way the clay will get in the hypodermic and clog it up," Poon reports. "The way the water will ooze up into the clay and soften it, making it impossible to tap with your little silver hammer and crack it open."

In the end, perseverance prevailed and the scene was filmed to perfection. As Poon points out, the world of the food stylist isn't as much about being able to cook.

"It's problem-solving...it's about seeing a problem and thinking, 'How am I going to solve that?'"

The spectacular dishes not only have to amaze the eye, they have to serve a more basic purpose as well.

"It all has to be edible," Poon says. "Because they might eat it and that might be the one magic screen moment when it goes into their mouth."

That one perfect take can't be ruined by a dish that is inedible, but also one that might be tainted by a dirty hypodermic.

"That's rule number one: beyond making it beautiful, beyond making it cinematic...try not to kill the actors."

One of the more memorable dishes proved a challenge not only for the food team but the actors as well. But in case anyone is worried about the tiny chicks from the ortolan dish in "Ko No Mono" (season two, episode eleven), rest assured that they were crafted out of marzipan.

"They were quite edible," actor Hugh Dancy says. "Janice is incredible...she had used little bits of dried spaghetti to get the crunch of the bones, and nuts and dried fruit inside to try and replicate the texture of what the innards might be."

For Dancy, the only issue with the scene was the size.

"They were quite large. They couldn't have been much smaller because they were baby birds, but still it was a substantial chunk of marzipan going into my mouth on every take."

While Hannibal might not think twice about serving such a controversial meal, it's tempting to wonder if anything would be off-limits for him.

José Andrés doesn't think so.

"He's gastronomically savvy," he says. "And I think he would treat every organ as a new opportunity to achieve perfection...lungs of a smoker? Perfect! They're already pre-smoked. He's so meticulous that I know he wouldn't let one body part go to waste."

FRANKLIN & TOBIAS

Asked if Hannibal is concerned with the well-being of his patients, Mads Mikkelsen is emphatic.

"Absolutely. I mean it depends on who...some of the patients are plain annoying, rude, dumb or banal and they will either end up on the streets or his table."

For Hannibal's patients, a healthy therapeutic relationship (and outright survival) depends on the interest they inspire in their health care provider. If you make him curious, you're likely to benefit from your sessions.

"He's an honest man," Mikkelsen says. "I don't think he ever told a lie ...he's always trying to cover up the truth but he's not telling a straight-forward lie and that goes with his emotions as well. If he likes something, he *likes* it; and if he hates it, he *hates* it. In that sense, he is full of empathy."

Bryan Fuller concurs.

"He is trying to get his patients closer to a truer version of themselves."

If you examine Hannibal's relationship with Will Graham, Lecter is trying to help his friend "become" the man he is meant to be and is "working under the assumption that Will Graham has all of the pieces to be a horrible killer," says Fuller. "So it's about trying to get him to come to a more honest place with his identity."

A vital question in the early stages of developing the series was one question: What happens when an unbridled individualist seeks a friend?

There are many mirrored relationships throughout the show, and the neurotic Franklin Froideveaux and his friendship with the burgeoning serial killer Tobias Budge provide a strong reflection for the Hannibal/Will Graham pairing.

[Above Left & Right] Franklin (Dan Fogler) and his reluctant best friend, Tobias Budge (Demore Barnes). Their short-lived friendship, which we see for the first time in season one, episode seven comes to a bloody end in episode eight. [Below] Will admires Tobias' handiwork.

The original intention was to feature Jame Gumb, better known as Buffalo Bill. But when rights issues prohibited his inclusion, Fuller and his writing team created Tobias Budge, a man who crosses paths with another serial killer in Hannibal but is a man in search of his own authentic experience—in this case, a violin strung with vocal cords.

This ghoulish concert recital started with a prosthetic character, but the team at Rocket Science VFX came in to assist.

"It was covered by quite a lot in shooting," Robert Crowther from Rocket Science VFX says. "That needed to be trimmed down because it was very graphic. But we did an effect of the wound closing back up and when [Tobias] is shoving the neck of the violin into the body."

Blueprints and production photography of Tobias' basement where he turned his victims into violin strings.

Tobias proved a worthy opponent and for the first time we were able to see Hannibal in a more vulnerable light.

RANDALL TIER

The "Harrisian" theme of transformation is clear in this character. This former patient of Lecter's had killed before but his desire to "become an animal" only happened when, as an adult, he fashioned a hydraulic suit out of the bones and hides of animals.

Hannibal takes a strong interest in Randall and urges him to become the animal he feels that he is beneath his human exterior, suffering from a kind of "humanity dysphoria". Part of Hannibal's desire is to nudge his patients to become a truer version of themselves, and as such part of his therapy with Tier is coaching him to indulge his homicidal impulses.

The attraction Hannibal feels for Tier, however, is different than the interest he holds for Graham. While Will's appetite for murder happens through external forces, his struggle is to come to terms with what *has* happened versus what he thinks he is capable of doing again. Tier's tastes, on the other hand, are a dramatic result of the existential muddle he wades through every day.

[Right] One of Randall Tier's (Mark O'Brien) victims found by Jack's team in season two, episode nine. The contrast between red and white, blood on snow, is yet another example of the striking cinematography that unpins the visuals of the whole show.

[Far Right] Concept designs for Tier's bite pattern.

"I think he saw, in Randall Tier, someone who could not reconcile how he felt on the inside and how he felt on the outside," Fuller says.

What Tier grapples with is analogous with transgenderism, in what Fuller admits is a "terrible, terrible, inappropriate metaphor". That said, the methods Hannibal applies to Tier in his dysphoric condition is comparable to those struggling with gender identification.

"[Hannibal] said that if on the inside you feel this way, then you have to embrace that," says Fuller. "So if Randall Tier was a transgendered patient who was feeling one gender on the outside and another on the inside and being able to bridge those genders through psychiatry, that would be an effective psychiatrist and somebody you would want as your therapist.

"That encouraging Tier to embrace what was on the inside came at a mortal price is of little consequence to Hannibal, who sees his treatment plan as the best available to aid his patient.

[Above] Concept artwork for Tier's suit. Designers created the jaw mechanism and even had to consider the way the claws splayed during an attack.

[Below] Early concept sketches by Jeff Vlaming, Co-Executive Producer and writer on the show.

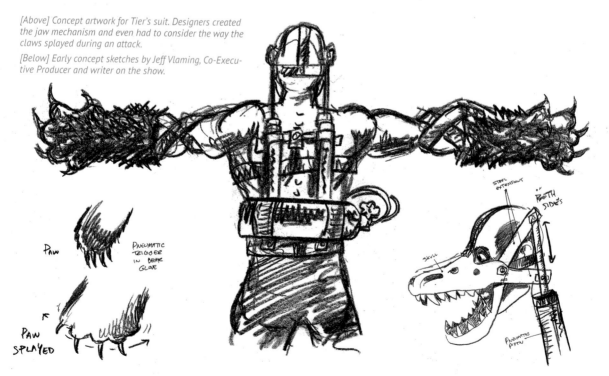

More advanced concepts for Tier's suit. After the sketch stage, designers moved onto 3D modelling and put in extra detail, like the ribs and hair, which give the silhouette [below] a more sinister, animalistic edge.

"It is so much more destructive," Fuller says, "and yet remaining true to the core of his patient's identity. So I think he was applying what he felt was the appropriate therapy to allow someone to get in touch with their truer self and an instance where you could argue that that therapy could be used on another patient in less extreme situations for a very healthy benefit."

Writing an episode about a man who struggles with the animal inside is one thing but, as one can imagine, making the exoskeleton of this "werewolf" story was daunting because of the expectations and the desire to produce a unique end product.

"No one really knew what it had to look like," Mindwarp FX's François Dagenais recalls. "We got some designs and I thought 'What can we do?' And then it took its own shape."

Fuller arrived to look at what Dagenais and his team invented and was smitten. Instead of a leather-stretched bone suit, they had created the symbiosis of man and animal that fit in neatly with the notion of transformation.

A visual compliment of the "transformation" theme in the show is the manner in which Will Graham reconstructs the crime scenes he visits, an empathic power he uses to great effect at the sight of Randall Tier's lakeside murder of an unsuspecting couple.

Robert Crowther from Rocket Science VFX states that a great deal of thought was given to these mental reconstructions from the start of the first season onward. Almost as much effort was spent deciding on specifically how not to do them.

"Will does these crime scene reconstructions and we did a lot of different things. We wanted to make sure that it didn't fall into any one standard way of doing

CHARGE SHEET

First Degree Murder of multiple
victims using a a cave bear skull
as the primary killing weapon

[Left] Jack comes face-to-face with what has become of Randall Tier. [Above] Concept designs for Tier's death tableau where he is given his ultimate wish - to become the animal within. [Above Right] Tier's arrest warrant citing the charge: 'First degree murder of multiple victims using a cave bear skull as the primary killing weapon.'

it, we wanted to try and do something different with it every time," he recalls. "A lot of television shows rely on those kinds of things where it is exactly 'this' and it becomes formulaic."

The Rocket Science team are always searching for a way to use the specific surroundings to augment the pendulum effect that wipes the scene clean of bodies and blood. Crowther sites the mushrooms from season one as a favourite, but Tier's murder of the two couples also displays a knowing knack for showing subtle reversals of time: the pendulum swipes behind Graham like a setting sun on the frozen lake, smoke from an extinguished fire gathers, descends and reignites the reassembled tent of chopped wood. Rocket Science used CG objects to reconstruct the wood for the fire and the result is far from formulaic, and pure *Hannibal*.

MARGOT & MASON VERGER

The Vergers each possess enough complicated psychological entanglements to pique Hannibal's interest.

While Margot lives a story that Hannibal finds compelling (enough that he tries to counsel her into a path of virtuous murder not unlike his motives for Will Graham), whereas Mason proves that similar raising at the hand of a sadistic patriarch can turn one into a predatory, gauche boor.

"He's also clumsy," Mikkelsen says. "He's not elegant or labyrinth in what he's doing. She's interesting, but

Hannibal can also use her to make them spin around Will even better."

Hannibal is fascinated with Mason because he is such a creature of his environment and, as a result, free from the social contracts that bind most of us in polite, if simmering, interpersonal relations.

"He is deplorable as a human being," Fuller says. "And for Hannibal it is interesting to break him down and study those pieces."

Ultimately, it is more of an intellectual exercise than his interactions with Margot Verger, for whom

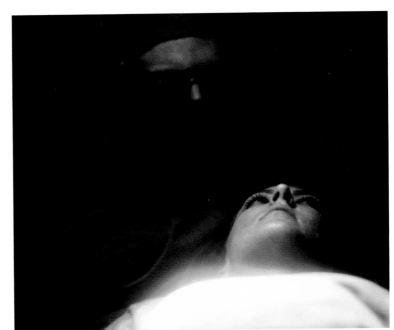

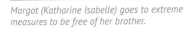

Margot (Katharine Isabelle) goes to extreme measures to be free of her brother.

Hannibal feels genuine compassion. He certainly doesn't see Mason that way.

Bryan continues, "he's such an example of all that is wrong with humanity that Hannibal Lecter is as fascinated with him as he is with Will Graham being an example of someone who is totally empathic and resonates with the world around him. Whereas Mason Verger is a bit of an island."

What to do, then, with such an island? Build a bridge or destroy the pier and burn all the ships? Considering Mason's propensity for poor manners, it is no surprise that Hannibal feeds him a psychotropic drug and convinces him to carve off pieces of his face and feed them to Will Graham's dogs before breaking his neck and transforming him into a quadriplegic.

"I felt pretty strongly that we should go a visual effects route," Anthony Patterson remembers. "Ultimately it was decided that they were going to attempt to go with prosthetics."

The prosthetics team was brought in to build the initial face mask, from the casting of the actor's face, and then sculpted away from that base. That was applied to actor Michael Pitt's face along with a dental prosthetic and he appeared on set ready to cut up his own face. Actually talking, however, was another matter.

[Above] One of Mason's (Michael Pitt) many psychological and physical tortures of his sister, from dressing the "meat man" in one of her suits (season two, episode ten), to giving her a forced hysterectomy to prevent a Verger heir from stealing his inheritance (season two, episode eleven).

You never heard that one from Miss Manners, did you?

"We had a lot of discussions early on," Anthony Patterson of Rocket Science VFX remembers. "It was during those first couple of meetings on that particular episode that we discussed different ways to achieve the look of him slicing his face open."

Budgetary concerns are always at the forefront of such conversations and, as a rule of thumb, practical effects are always cheaper than CG. So the decision was made to fit Mason Verger (as played by Michael Pitt) with a prosthetic.

The actor's ability to speak when fitted with the dental appliance made for a post-production scramble. "In the end, all his lines were dubbed and all the action of him opening his mouth and speaking was done with CGI effects in post," Patterson says. Luckily they had performed a 3D scan of the actor's face before the scene was shot, so they were able to "achieve a level of realism in those shots that...you really don't question. It looks like a guy cutting pieces of his face off and eating it."

[Above & Right] On-set production stills of Mason's punishment prior to the special effects contribution.

BEDELIA DU MAURIER

We don't know much about Bedelia Du Maurier but what we do learn about her often comes out in the therapy sessions with Lecter. Those one-on-ones tease out information as to their background as colleagues and Lecter's involvement with "saving" her from an attacker. In much of the same way that Graham feels responsible for Abigail Hobbs, so too does Hannibal for Bedelia.

Their relationship is deeper than that, however. Du Maurier has retired and stopped seeing patients with the exception of Hannibal. There is an undercurrent of danger to their sessions; that Hannibal is capable of anything and Bedelia knows it. But is her interest in him purely self-protection?

"I think Bedelia wants to understand Hannibal as a man and a monster," Fuller says. "And I think she has never seen or encountered anyone like him."

Fuller contends that she has a "greed" for "personal edification".

"She wants to know, she wants to understand. She is so fascinated with the human condition, like Hannibal, and having not encountered anyone like him before, she is determined to learn how he works in a way that will help her greater understand humanity as a whole.

"She is an interesting character because I think she is the best therapist for Hannibal Lecter, but she's also somebody whose curiosity is so great that it can allow her to overlook certain legal issues surrounding her patient," he says with a laugh.

Given the circumstances, Bedelia's dedication to her patient is commendable. She seems to exist in the universe to show the positive side of psychiatry—that happens by default when the doctor in question isn't a vainglorious manipulator (Dr. Chilton) or game-playing eater of human flesh. Bedelia has a fixed moral center but her allegiances to the doctor-patient bond come into question when, in season two, she steps into the light and helps Will understand that he is right in thinking the worst of Hannibal Lecter.

Fuller explains, "in that situation, it was dawning on her exactly how deep Hannibal's humanity, or lack thereof, ran within him."

Fuller further suggests that when she realized there was a shared experience between her and Graham, in that they had both been subject to the same psychological manipulations and both occupied a perilous situation as a result, that she felt that she had no other choice but to reach out to him.

"I think it was just her humanity to reach out to another person and say, 'I believe you. You are not alone.' And that was an honest gesture on her part, because she felt for the man, she empathized with him, and could see the madness in his situation and simply wanted to offer a tiny bit of support in a very, very dark time."

THE COPYCAT

From the moment that Will Graham sees the body of Cassie Boyle mounted on a stag head in Hibbing, Minnesota, with her lungs removed, he knows that it is not the work of The Minnesota Shrike. Graham is quick to understand not only that this killer doesn't have the same "love" for his victims as the Shrike, but also that he has presented this "field kabuki" in an effort to guide him, to teach him. Only later does he decide that this scene has been provided as a "negative" so that good Will Graham can see the "positive" of the real Shrike.

An early decision in staging this open field murder scene was whether to use a prosthetic body or an actress. Director David Slade had concerns that a silicone body would look exactly like a rubber dummy, and as important as realism is in any episode, as this was the pilot it was imperative that the audience not be pulled out of the scene by spotting the zipper down the back of the monster suit.

However, they opted for the prosthetic for practical reasons. As François Dagenais says, while the aim for an authentic body was alluring, there remained

[Right & Bottom Right] One of Patti Podesta's early concept pieces for the stag-head tableau and the 3D rendering of the same, created with exact measurements to allow the team to accurately recreate the scene.

concerns about putting an actress through such a trial. "It would have been very uncomfortable, that was the main concern," Dagenais says. "And also not having somebody there means you can keep shooting and not have to worry about the actress getting up to take a break."

Dagenais and his team molded the body of a background performer, then molded the head of the actress.

"This body had to be articulated because we saw her laying backwards and then we saw her later on straight on the slab.

"The limbs are all articulated and it was a full-size silicone body so the weight also helped the look of the body lying on the antlers."

When The Copycat decided to mount the body of Marissa Schurr on antlers in Garret Jacob Hobbs'

trophy room, Dagenais reused the body of Cassie Boyle but with slight alterations.

"Every time the Cassie body was there it had a wig with her head looking toward the floor so we never really saw her," Dagenais recalls. "When it was time to actually see her face, they used the real actress."

What of The Copycat and his motivations? Is there anything as easy as a "reason" for his actions?

"There's something too banal about having an excuse for what he does," Mads Mikkelsen says. "'Oh, so this happened to you when you were a kid and that's why you're doing all this stuff.' We don't want to go there."

Those looking for answers won't find any, but you will find hints.

"We want to make it as enigmatic as we can, but then put little pebbles out there that can make people curious."

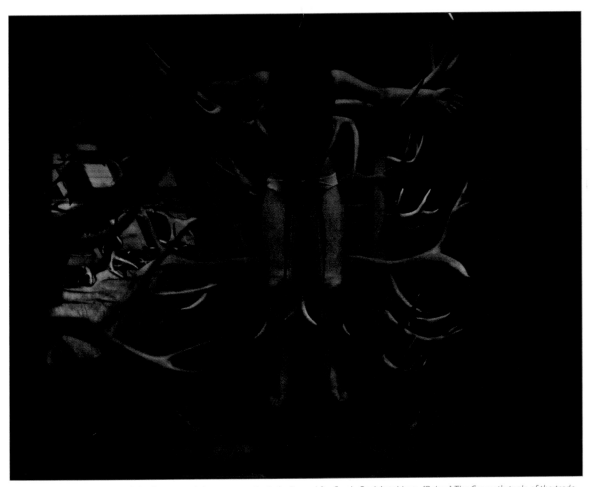

[Above] Marissa Shurr, victim of the Copycat and the same prosthetic body used for Cassie Boyle's tableau. [Below] The Copycat's tools of the trade.

While some might think of his actions as those of a maniac, Mikkelsen doesn't think it is that simple.

"I don't think he's a psychopath," he says. "He's just a reverse person. He is a fallen angel in that he sees beauty where the rest of us are seeing evil. Where we see something horrendous, he sees something beautiful there. It's kind of a reverse, mirror image of our concept of life or beauty."

A man who sees the potential in every day in such an ecstatic, albeit gruesome, fashion is light and unaffected by the everyday worries that plague the rest of us.

"He's probably a character that is the happiest I've ever played. There's absolutely nothing that I bring

to him that has a depressing edge to it. He is a man who seizes the moment every single day. 'Today was interesting, tomorrow can be even more interesting'."

While rudeness is a simple lack of couth, Mikkelsen believes that Hannibal sees banality as an even greater sacrilege.

"Banality is a sin because he does see the beauty of life and he wants life at its utmost to be perfection. There is no reason to listen to boring music, you may as well listen to fantastic music, or drink a fantastic glass of wine. And for that reason, banality is a sin.

"That means you do not live your life fully, you do not grasp and embrace the moment every day. And to him, that's not living at all."

GLASGOW SMILE

As one might imagine from the name, the act of slicing someone's mouth at the corners so that it resembles a ghastly grin is thought to have originated in Scotland, especially with the menacing Glasgow Razor Gangs of the 1920s and 30s. It is also known as one of the indignities visited upon the body of Elizabeth Short, whose bisected remains were found in a field in Los Angeles in the late 1940s and dubbed The Black Dahlia.

In the original incarnation, the wounds were small but the gruesome grin is achieved by beating the victim whose painful contortions tear the cheeks back closer to the ears. Georgia Madchen visits this upon her friend Beth LeBeau in "Buffet Froid" (season one, episode ten) but this is the least complicated in terms of prosthetic work. Make-up was applied to the actress playing LeBeau but more involved work was required for the untimely end of the conniving Dr. Sutcliffe.

[Above Left & Right] Dr. Sutcliffe (John Benjamin Hickey) before and after Hannibal has decided his fate.

[Below] Dr. Sutcliffe's gruesome tableau and one of the most striking visuals in the series. [Right] Production still showing the motion capture points on Mads' face.

[Above] The 3D set plans for Dr. Sutcliffe's office, allowing the team to plan the bloody scene with minimal expense.

"It was a fake head," François Dagenais reports. "Because it was so extreme."

The radical Glasgow Smile of Dr. Sutcliffe, with the aggressive cuts up over the ears and ripped-down jaw, brought out the best in Dagenais' team. Most would think that such a sight wouldn't generate humour, but gallows humour is a necessity for people working on a set like *Hannibal*. As a result, the sawed-open head of Dr. Sutcliffe was knighted with a nickname.

"We called him 'The Pez Head'."

Other Glasgow Smiles were created with make-up works that were applied directly onto the faces of the actors, but Lecter's extra-credit work on Dr. Sutcliffe required an equally Herculean amount of work from the prosthetics team.

Another creepy effect is the moment where Hannibal, after carving up Dr. Sutcliffe's face, is confronted by Georgia whose ability to identify faces is impaired by the Cotard's Syndrome from which she suffers. Instead of just a smear where Hannibal's face should be, Rocket Science worked to achieve a more eerie effect that might better represent what a sufferer of this syndrome might experience.

"It's a subtle thing we did where there's still some shape and sockets," Robert Crowther says. "We even did a test where we did the Hannibal grill from the movies, but that was one where Bryan Fuller said, 'We don't really want to reference the movies per se.' And he was saving it, as well, for season two."

[Left] The black dots on Mads Mikkelsen's face during filming are motion caption points. They allow for the Rocket Science team to apply the 'blurring' effect to his face so the viewer can experience how Georgia's condition affects her view of others.

JACK CRAWFORD

LAURENCE FISHBURNE

A man on a mission, Jack Crawford is constantly straddling worlds—whether it is corralling Will's empathic gifts and enjoying fine dining with Lecter, or the subtler tragedies of life at home and the brutal demands of a high-stress job. Crawford knows that to survive he must navigate the delicate balance between the noble and the profane. This dichotomy is well represented in his wardrobe, described by costume designer Christopher Hargadon as "one that has one eye on style and another on function.

"Because his colour palette was different, we could use coloured shirts. I tried to make him look sophisticated and not garish. I wanted him to have a little style but have a little context with the FBI."

Fishburne's attraction to the show, and working with Bryan Fuller, could easily be applied to the character he plays: complex layers of subtext in the characters and the storytelling.

"One of the wonderful things about our show," Fishburne says, "is we have the wonderful and macabre mind of Bryan Fuller at work, but at the same time he also takes great care to infuse everything with two and three and four layers of sub-text and emotional content. There's layers and layers and layers and layers behind everyone."

Fishburne is equally amazed by Fuller's desire to weave relatable tragedy into the ghoulish extravagance at play. It is surprising to have a storyline that features a banal but omnipresent killer like cancer in a horror setting like *Hannibal*, but it is quite another feat to have it dramatized with such quotidian heartbreak.

"The idea of using Jack's whole story about his wife and the cancer," Fishburne says. "To introduce that as an emotional state for our character, it's fascinating. And gives us a great deal of stuff to play with. And when you think about how he's constructed the friendship between Will Graham and Hannibal Lecter, where Hannibal's great desire is to become friends... that is diabolically wonderful."

THE FBI ENVIRONS

It makes sense that the surrounding environment at the FBI would be just as serious and focused as the man who runs the show.

Caroline Dhavernas puts it best when she talks about the anxiety the FBI offices inspire.

"I used to walk onto these sets and go, 'Oh my God, this set is going to eat me up.' I think that says a lot about how cool they are. These sets make you feel like 'what will Hannibal do to you'. They're very constructed, very severe and very dark."

The design language for the FBI is very much of the Brutalist school, a Modernist architectural movement from the mid-1950s to 1970s that gained popularity with government bodies across the globe. Buildings comprised of exposed concrete to create the look of a fortified base seem like a natural fit for institutional structures.

"Quantico in Virginia is Concrete Brutalist," production designer Matthew Davies says. "It's not quite as flavorful or interesting as the architecture we have on the show, but it is of that area."

Davies says that he always thinks of the 1950s and 1960s to be the Golden Era of the CIA, the FBI, and the authoritarian structure of America.

"To create a hybrid of that, to update it and give it a contemporary feel so it becomes what people associate with the architecture of authority—its weight, its low ceilings—it's oppressive and feels like a gargantuan mask sitting on their shoulders."

A specific influence for Davies is the Brutalism of Venetian architect Carlo Scarpa. His combinatorial use of finishes such as marble and wood is something Davies mimicked in the FBI sets and other sets on the show.

Set design for Jack's office and the surrounding corridors of the FBI building.

"We try to create a hybrid of iconic approaches to architecture," Davies notes.

Director of Photography James Hawkinson notes that while lighting on a set such as Hannibal's office is constantly changing to align with the doctor's whims, the FBI lab is lit in a consistent manner.

"Because it is the safest place for the audience to be... so it is one place where the lighting doesn't change as much. It is the one place the audience should feel slightly familiar and comfortable in."

It is interesting to note that only on a show like *Hannibal* would a morgue be the safest place for the audience.

As for the effect that production design has on performance, Fishburne has a sense that it is unavoidable.

"I'm sure that, on some level, it effects you. Environment always effects you. But again, how? It's a really subtle thing."

Just as subtle is the shifting relationship between Jack Crawford and Will Graham.

"You have to have Will Graham central and then an angel on one shoulder and a devil on the other," Bryan Fuller suggests. "One of them is Jack Crawford and the other is Hannibal Lecter, and over the course of the series they switch positions."

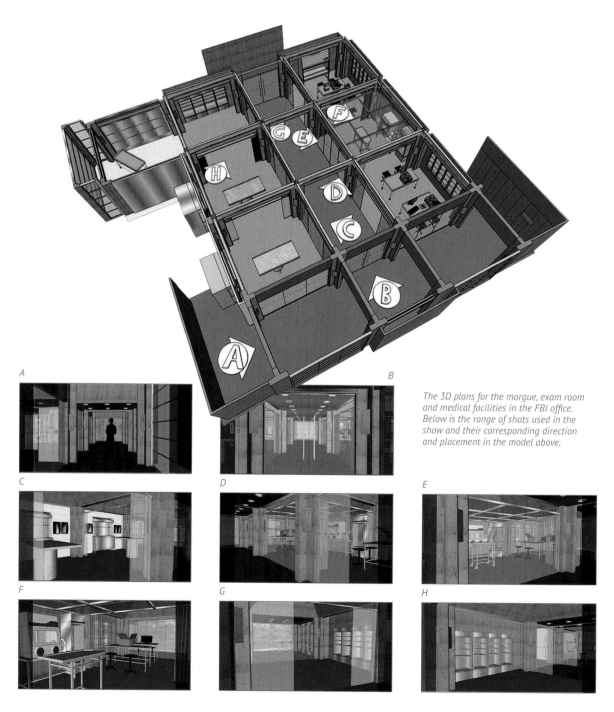

The 3D plans for the morgue, exam room and medical facilities in the FBI office. Below is the range of shots used in the show and their corresponding direction and placement in the model above.

How else to explain why Crawford is so willing to push Graham into places that are potentially very dangerous for him, and warned against by his psychiatrist Lecter?

"It's hard to tell who is more invested in Will's psychological well-being—Hannibal Lecter or Jack Crawford, because they're both pulling at him like he's taffy," says Fuller.

He also submits that there are times in both the first and second seasons where Jack is the villain, if you were to break it down purely by what is best for Will Graham.

"Jack would be the bad guy in certain scenarios," he continues. "And Hannibal, who is trying to buttress Will's psychology and support him and is warning against involvement with criminal profiling because

[Bottom] Director David Semel (center) and cinematographer James Hawkinson (left) on set during filiming of season two, episode four "Takiawase".

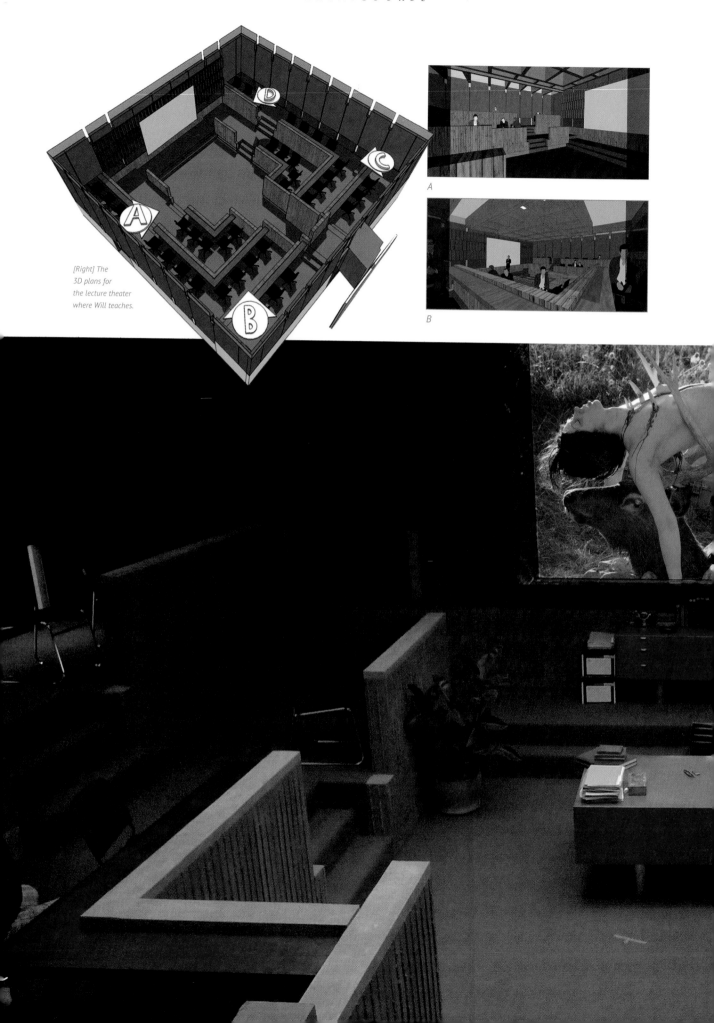

[Right] The
3D plans for
the lecture theater
where Will teaches.

A

B

C

D

it is a very dark and dangerous rabbit hole that Will could disappear into."

Some of those scenes, if taken out of context, would suggest that Lecter is in Will's corner and Crawford is not.

"Hannibal is Will's champion," Fuller explains, "and trying to guide him out of the briar patch while Jack Crawford, on the other hand, keeps throwing him back into it."

When asked how Crawford views Graham, Fishburne says that it is a complicated vision.

"He's certainly a colleague, he's certainly somebody he has to look after, he's certainly somebody who he just admires and treasures in many ways. He values Will a great deal because of his ability to do what he does. And at the same time he's an asset and a tool. And they're friends...it's very strange. It's very layered."

PHYLLIS "BELLA" CRAWFORD

The layering continues into Jack Crawford's relationship with his wife, Bella. If the literature of Thomas Harris is known for blending the details of police procedurals with the terrors of the modern world, Fuller's *Hannibal* might be just as well-regarded for the ability to balance elegant horror with the subtleties of everyday human relationships. In the case of Jack and Bella, it is a union that offers a great deal of emotional resonance for the audience.

A great deal of that comes from Fuller pulling the tertiary mention of Crawford's wife dying of cancer from the literature and developing it into a full subplot

in the series. Even more comes from the fact that Gina Torres, who plays Crawford's wife, is Fishburne's partner in real life. As such, it is impossible for it not to inform their relationship on screen.

"We've been married for twelve years," he says. "We've known each other for twenty years. She lost a parent to cancer, so she knows that journey. I've lost people to the disease so you know...you just dive in. It's rare that you get an opportunity to play something so real and so much a part of every human being's experience. There isn't a person on the planet who hasn't been touched by cancer. That's where it lives."

The wilting flower that Bella becomes as she struggles with cancer through the series is, again, reflected in the production design, with the Crawford's bedroom draped in the naturalistic imagery of rare orchids.

"We printed all the papers using 18th century etchings of orchids from a library in Paris," says Davies.

The imperative to avoid banalities of space and create the exceptional continued into Bella's hospital room.

"We did her hospital room in a more refined brutalist aesthetic, more like an early 80s Californian brutalism with travertine marble and polished concrete," says Davies. "It was designed to look almost like a chapel."

ALANA BLOOM

In a genre that can often be equally brutal and dismissive of female characters, *Hannibal*'s Alana Bloom is an exception. No mere appendage or damsel-in-distress, Alana is a fully-rounded character with desires and contradictions. But in a show as visually and thematically heavy as this one, she does represent an important center to the slaughter that surrounds her.

"Sometimes I was thinking, 'Where is the light in this?'" Caroline Dhavernas (*Wonderfalls, The Pacific, The Tulse Luper Suitcases*) recalls. "'How do I feel what I am saying?' Because it is all very cerebral, and the intention is not always really said...but my character is the exception at times. She is, I think, the heart of the show. She is the lighter one, she is more honest, to the point and direct."

[Left] Alana is a fierce defender of Will Graham and, ultimately to her detriment, of Hannibal Lecter. When the team comes under investigation by Kade Prurnell (Cynthia Nixon, far left), Alana is the voice of reason.

[Above] Alana escorting Abigail back to her home in an attempt to assist her in remembering her father's crimes.

The emotional compass she embodies is critical in a show that is, as she notes, comprised of characters analyzing each other in a way that is almost more interrogation than conversation.

"They're always sitting one in front of the other, analyzing each other and assessing a lot on what they're feeling," she says. "And Alana does say it at some point: 'I always assess what I'm feeling instead of acting upon my feelings.'"

"As Hannibal says, 'It's the safest way.'"

Safety and stability, or at least the promise of each, provides the base for the initial attraction that Will Graham has for Alana, while her interest in him is purely personal and not remotely clinical.

"Actually, Will says about Alana in the second episode of the first season that he appreciates they've never been alone in a room together," Hugh Dancy says. "He's deeply grateful that she's actually shown not too much interest in him, especially professional interest. She hasn't quietly taken notes so she can publish a paper on his bizarre mentality."

Dhavernas concurs. In discussions with Bryan Fuller, it became clear that she would question him about his well-being far and above any other inquiry.

"And that is what Alana has been about," she says. "She has been one of the rare ones to actually have his well-being at heart and to think about that before having any interest in what he can do for her."

That is not to say that she is above any professional curiosity. "She knows that she could be doing what Jack Crawford is doing with him, using him as a tool. To do good, but to use him nonetheless."

She also knows that she could fall for him romantically and want to fix him. Dhavernas says of Alana, "She's very smart in that way to know what her patterns are, what she could do with this guy, but choose not to go there."

As Dancy points out, when Graham turns to her more as he is suffering his breakdown near the end of the first season, it is likely just as inspired by the encephalitis as his crumbling health.

"I think you could argue that if Will were a bit more stable, he actually never would have opened up the romantic avenue in that relationship.

"And equally…when Hannibal starts his affair with Alana, he's clearly doing it in part to position himself better to blackmail Will with it. I mean, there's some personal feeling in there as well, but I think he knows exactly what he's doing."

It is no surprise that an intelligent woman could be duped by such a consummately evil man as Hannibal, which would lead her to an understandable, if not rational, conclusion.

"The Will relationship was more passionate and messy," says Dhavernas. "And this one [with Hannibal] is more rational."

It is no surprise then that, despite Hannibal and Alana knowing each other for some time before the period covered in the show, a trigger is required for them to initiate a romantic bond. In the case of the second season and in the wake of Will's apparent role as a serial killer, they are joined by mourning.

"Alana is convinced that he did it," Dhavernas says. "But he did it because he had encephalitis. So she's there with him and doesn't judge because, for her, he was pushed in that direction. So in season two she starts off knowing that there is no possible way that this love story is going to go anywhere. In my mind, she's trying to have a grown-up relationship that makes sense. And I think she and Hannibal are close because they have to let go of Will in their minds. They have to grieve."

Many who walk through the grieving process find solace in a romantic yearning, along with a more primal one.

Dhavernas explains, "It's weird to say that a funeral can make you horny, but it was that idea of 'Let's live. We have this time now to live and we're burying this friend that we both had.' I think they become close together in this truth and in this strong, intense feeling."

After considering a relationship with Will Graham—a man whose facility with social cues is suspect even without the effect of encephalitis—it is understandable that Alana Bloom would consider involvement with Hannibal Lecter as the "adult" choice.

"I think that's how it all happened...little did she know at the time who Hannibal was."

Some may view Hannibal's interest in Alana as more strategic than romantic and with good reason. He is a man who does not cross his legs without considering the ramifications or mapping out an exit strategy. But the man who portrays Lecter doesn't see it in such a clear-cut fashion.

"You can always discuss whether Hannibal takes advantage of the situation or if it just happens," Mads Mikkelsen says. "It's very hard to know when it comes to Hannibal...but again, there's an honesty. He likes her, he wants her, he desires her for the situation. And tomorrow he might not. But it's always honest."

KATZ, PRICE & ZELLER

A leader is only as good as his team and Crawford is fortunate to have as dedicated a unit as Beverly Katz, Jimmy Price and Brian Zeller. The importance of a strong line-up in the field extends beyond crime scene investigation and out into the audience as well.

"If they're closer to us, they're closer to the audience," Fishburne says. "If the audience feels like any member of this team is in peril, that's a good thing."

That the dynamic among the team is well-defined from the outset is a testament to the work of the actors Aaron Abrams and Scott Thompson, but special attention is paid to Hettienne Park, for the skill she brought to the part (Park is a "really smart actor," Fishburne says) which left a noticeable hole in

[Above] The trio investigating Eldon Stammets' (Aidan Devine) mushroom garden. [Below Right] The horrible task of processing Will's house begins.

84

the team beneath Crawford and the cast of the show.

"Considering the nature of what our show is, people get killed," Fishburne notes. "We were just sad that she was going, straight up and down. I was just bummed that she wasn't going to be around anymore."

As noticeable as the loss was, of course, the manner in which she left us.

"From an artistic point-of-view," François Dagenais remembers. "That was a lot of fun."

While trying to solve a series of horrific crimes, and satisfy her own curiosity, Katz made the fatally rude mistake of nosing around Hannibal's basement. And in Lecter's twisted but consistent logical assessment, the punishment and display of her remains was consistent with the level of her sin.

While Park's dedication to her craft and performance as Katz inspired great feelings on the set, she was similarly devoted and impressive when it came time to create the body that would become the starting point for the *Body Worlds*-inspired tableau in the observatory.

Normally, Dagenais would call in a body double to create the cast from the neck down, the actor would come in for the head cast, and both would be married for the final product. Not so for Hettienne Park.

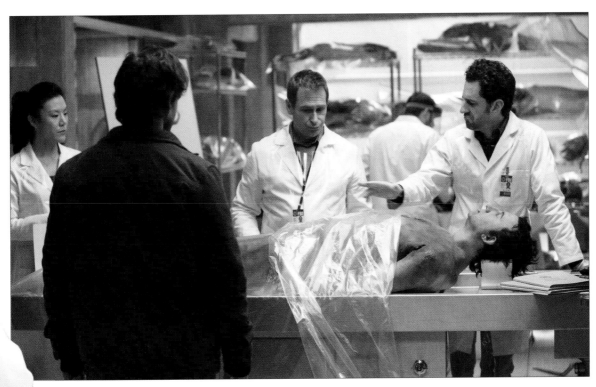

[Left & Above] The team dismantle and examine the Human Totem Pole from season one, episode nine "Trou Normand".

"For the Beverly body, she was right into it," Dagenais reports. "'I want to do that!'"

The process of creating the final sliced remains required a certain amount of "Method" work on the part of the prosthetic team.

"What I wanted to do was re-create a body of Beverly with all the organs and everything in it and physically slice it with a band saw like Hannibal would have."

"And that's what we did."

Dagenais and his team made a full body replica of Beverly Katz, bisected it and then filled it with the appropriate organs and used a saw to shave off layers.

"Then the actual detail work starts," Dagenais remembers. "You go in on each side of the slabs and put in the detail."

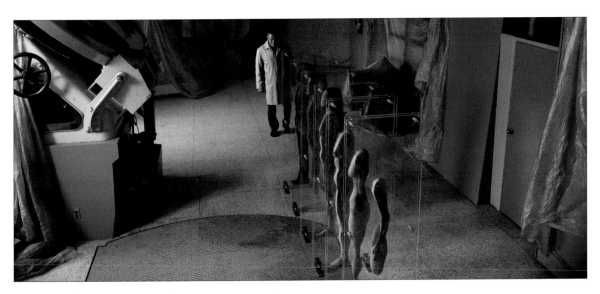

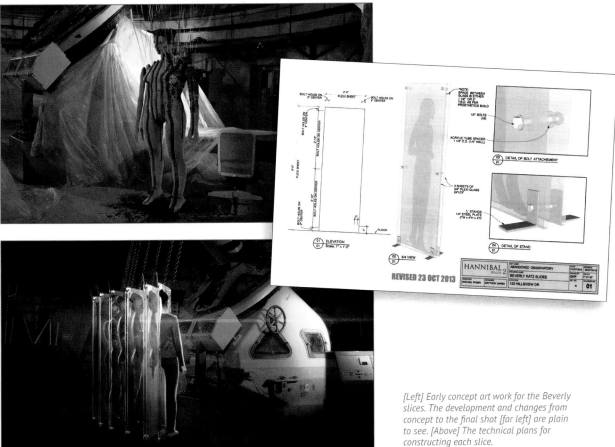

[Left] Early concept art work for the Beverly slices. The development and changes from concept to the final shot [far left] are plain to see. [Above] The technical plans for constructing each slice.

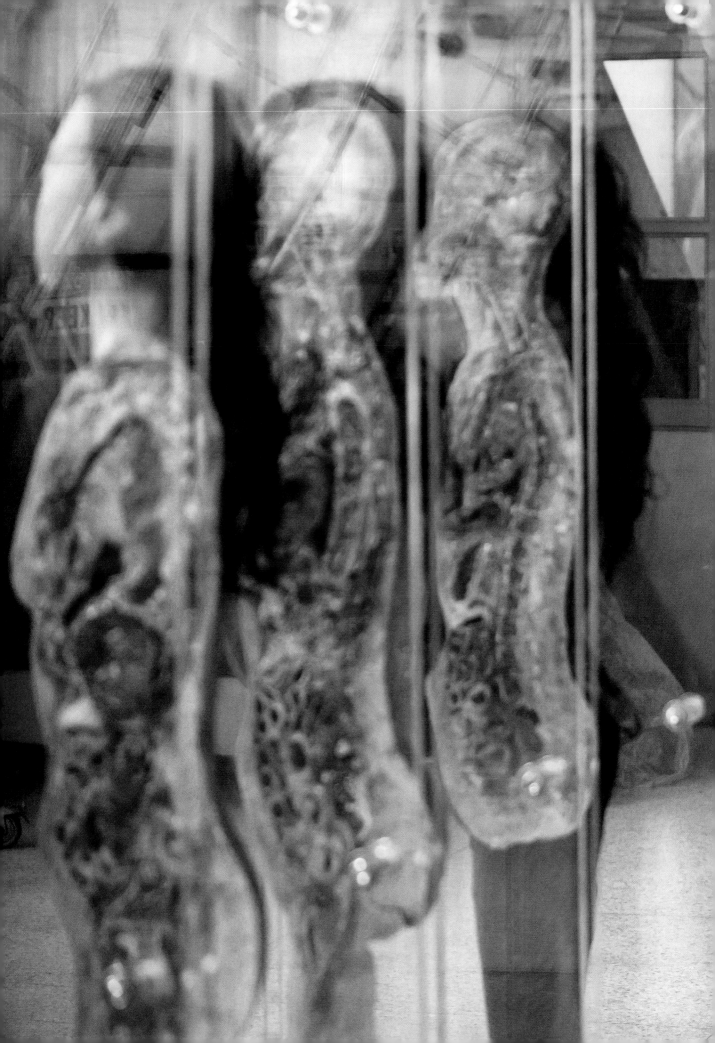

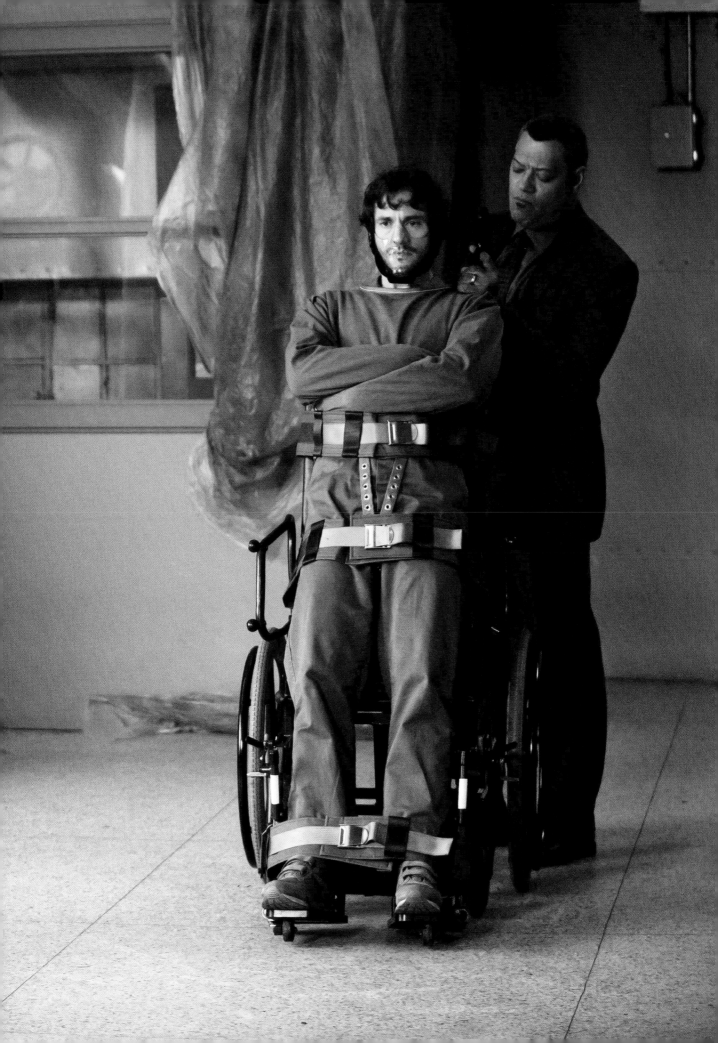

on the whole universe. While many people might wonder about the iconic performances of the main characters we now see on *Hannibal*, the same concern must also be paid to the supporting players. What reason is there to include Freddie Lounds if not to take a fresh angle with the character?

"So to have her in that role as a paparazzo of criminal investigation," was not enough, Fuller says. "We needed to have those levels in order to not just outwardly hate her and cringe when she's on the screen."

Another reason for the depth is that it is dictated by the format.

"It's television as opposed to the movies," Fuller points out. Even if you are dealing with a small "v" villain, if there isn't a genuine connection or level of sympathy between the character and the audience, then the viewers don't want to see as much of them.

"And since it's television, you're obligated to," Fuller notes.

"Also, as a writer, even if I'm writing a terrible character, I want to be able to understand them and

like them and appreciate their point of view on the world. Otherwise I can't write them as well."

For a shocking point of view, you would have to go back to the shooting of Dr. Frederick Chilton to find as shocking a turn of events as when confronted with the burning remains of Freddie Lounds, strapped to a wheelchair and set ablaze before being shoved down an underground parking ramp. Not only did it challenge the canon timeline, it also paid homage to a similar scene in Michael Mann's adaptation of *Red Dragon*, in the 1986 film *Manhunter*.

The scene, in the context of the series, provides more questions than answers. In the original literature, there is little doubt who killed Lounds and why. In the series, we're left with many serious questions about the transforming character of Will Graham and whether we believe he is capable of such an atrocity in his apparent change from light to dark.

When Lounds' body is later repurposed as the Grave Shiva (likely by a benefactor, as agreed upon by both Graham and Alana Bloom), we are treated to another bravura murder set piece and another meditation on the meaning of darkness.

In a very practical sense, darkness was a concern for director David Slade, who returned to direct this second season episode, "Kō No Mono". He and director of photography James Hawkinson had discussions about not only how darkness looks but how it should feel; about darkness not just as a shade but as an idea.

"And about the levels of darkness and when to be dark," Slade recalls. "Sometimes it's practical, as with the Grave Shiva. You'll see that it's incredibly backlit so it falls very much into shadow so you don't see as much. You see a shape, and you see the contrast and you feel like you're looking at something very specific but actually there's very little detail there because of the shadow."

Slade further explains his motivation for keeping details shrouded in dark, and it's not just to create a sense of foreboding.

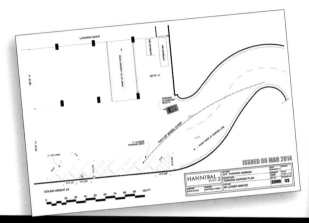

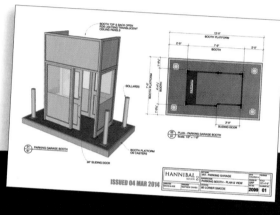

[Below] Everything on a set must be planned and measured perfectly, right down to the parking attendant booth and angle of approach for Freddie's flaming wheelchair.

"It invites you to lean forward and look closer if you dare," he says. "Jim has a very philosophical outlook as well, which is part and parcel of our show. He and I will have discussions not only about filmmakers and films past but also about philosophy, and what form of darkness this philosophy is—whether its redemptive, whether its damning. And then how far the darkness will go. So darkness is a big part of looking, because when your eyes can't see, your brain has to make up the rest."

As for the feeling of the graveyard set and the further darkness it dares the viewer to look into, Slade is very clear.

"We were in a graveyard. That wasn't a set; that was a real graveyard."

Darkness was a consideration for François Dagenais as well, but for his work it was more about the practicality of using the same piece twice, along with how to best make a silicone body look like it had

undergone a full burn. "We had to use this one for two scenes also," Dagenais remembers. "We had to use it for the burnt body of Freddie Lounds in the morgue and the post-exhumation with the hole in her head and in the Shiva position."

Dagenais and his team started with a body mould that they already had in the shop and constructed the silicone body with armature.

"We did the burnt body of Freddie with body joints that were opposable," Dagenais reports. Once they completed the shot in the FBI morgue, they brought the piece back to the shop and altered the head.

"Poked a big hole in it for the third eye," he says. "And we went to set and tied her up in position."

Working on many of the different hero pieces on *Hannibal* can prove a challenge, but Dagenais remembers that the work on the Grave Shiva body went smoothly.

"Once we're down to already having a mould—we've done bodies all season long so we know how the armatures work and how to put it together—the biggest thing is already having a mould. And the fact that she was burnt...again, it comes down to just creativity in terms of making the burn look nice.

"It was nice and light, compared to the horse one or the Tree Man."

[Below] The team prepare the Shiva for shooting. [Below left & right] An early concept sketch of the Shiva and the dental records used to convince the world of Freddie's demise. [Bottom] Close up detail shots of parts of Freddie's burnt body.

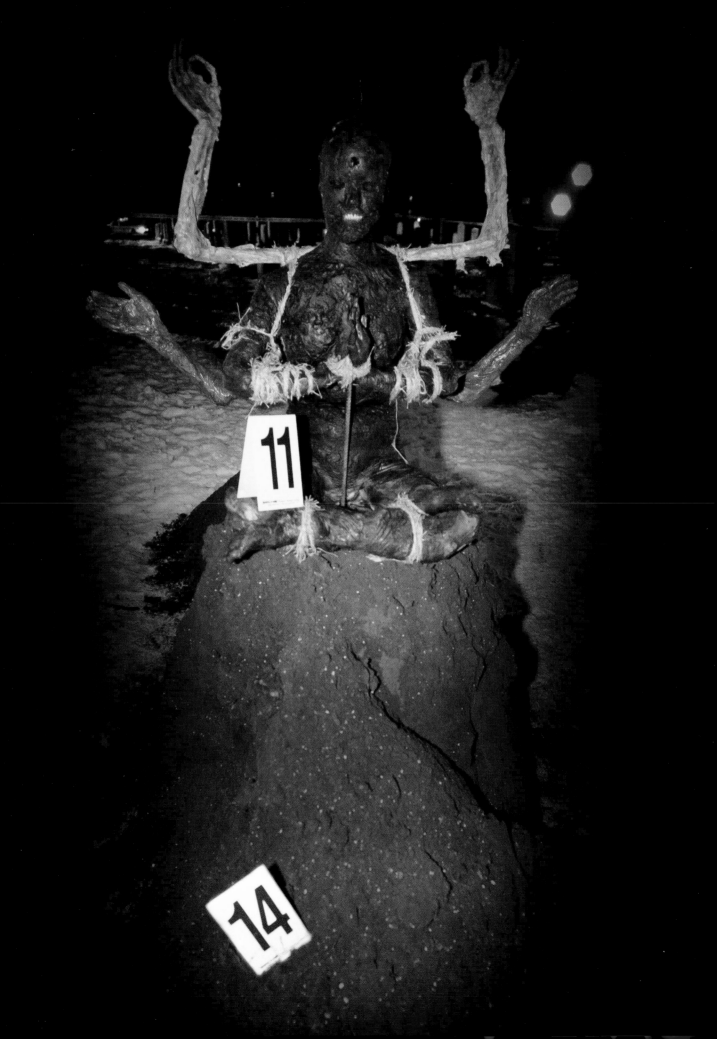

EYE OF GOD

One of Fishburne's favourite murder scenes was The Eye of God (seen on the next page in a pre-production still). The use of prosthetic bodies for this artful arrangement would not have allowed for the same level of realism and emotional impact.

"Forty-plus human bodies," Fishburne says. "They warmed the bottom of the floor for the background artists so they wouldn't succumb to the cold. And you walk into that room and you're hit immediately with all the scent of human flesh and the pheromones that are coming off everybody and all you want to do is lay down and go to sleep with them."

The full idea of the scene wasn't clear from the outset.

"Bryan did want it to be in a silo," Matthew Davies says. "And the eye came from a conference call we had

[Above & Below] Discovery and recovery of the 'rejected' victims—those who did not fit into the mural's color palette.

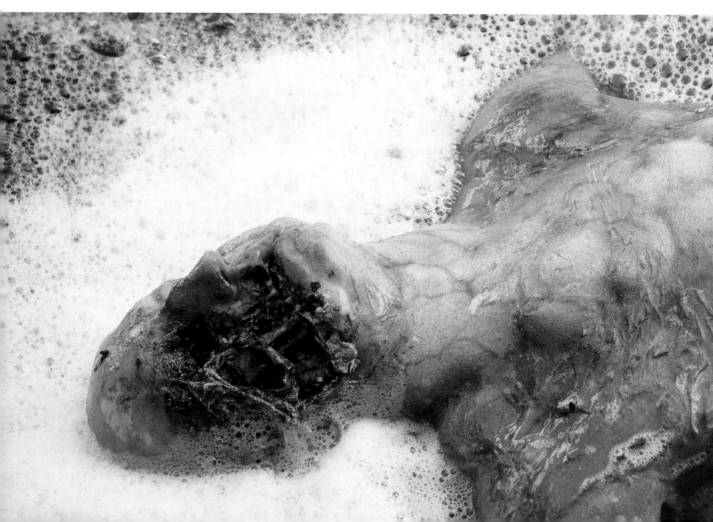

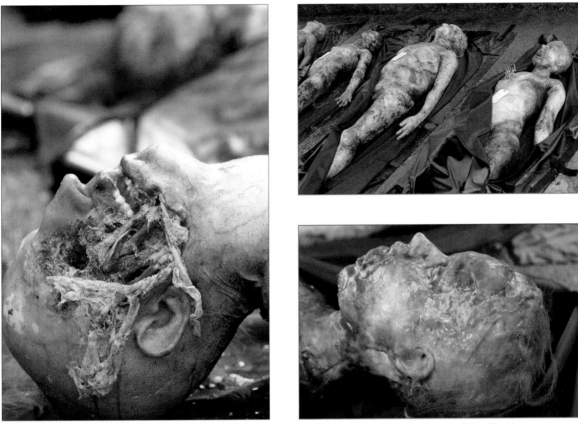

[Above] Close-ups of the prosthetic work. These bodies had to look like they had been submerged in a river for several days, if not longer.

where we stumbled upon a Busby Berkeley set still whilst we were Skyping."

Fuller latched onto the notion of using a style appropriated from a glitzy pre-World War Two musical and remixing it for his grisly purposes. He also liked the idea of the arranged bodies looking like an eye.

"So the idea became much more rich and developed as a consequence," Davies says.

To better prepare for the layout of background artists, Davies and his team put together a mock-up of the scene in a program called form Z, 3D modeling software used for architectural design as well as animation and rendering. The immediate benefits of such an approach was to allow precise positioning

of bodies as opposed to a free-for-all on the days of shooting.

"In form Z, you take human forms and you manipulate them," Davies says. "You lay them in order [for the production] to know exactly how we wanted them to lie so it wasn't just left to chance."

There are various levels of modeling available in the software, from rough work to broadcast-quality imagery. The mock-up Davies and company created was the crudest level of rendering. The highest quality may have provided an alternative to the production if the live shoot hadn't worked out so well.

"We could have done that whole thing without using real bodies," Davies submits. But even the finest 3-D

[Below] A pre-production shot of the forty-plus bodies which make up Umber's eye.

[Above] An aerial shot of the set and construction of the eye.

rendering can't produce the kind of sinister magic of over thirty human bodies huddled together on the floor, either for the audience or the actors on set.

The modeling software also provided the necessary palette to map the background actors not just for place-setting but also to better mimic the fibrous, marbled look of the ciliary zone of the iris of the human eye. That both technology and human endurance came together to complete one of the most stunning murder tableaus of the series so far is a testament to not only programming finesse but also to the dedication of the background artists employed for the two-day shoot.

Anthony Patterson recalls the dedication required of the background artists needed to obtain the arresting visual, saying that they were asked to lie mostly nude for two days of shooting.

"And remember what position they were in if they had to get up."

Patterson and Rocket Science FX used visual effects to cast any unwanted nudity into shadow and provide any subtle final touches.

"There was a lot of [visual effects work], in those scenes, making people look dead," Patterson says.

[Below] The plans and shot designs for such an elaborate and complicated visual.

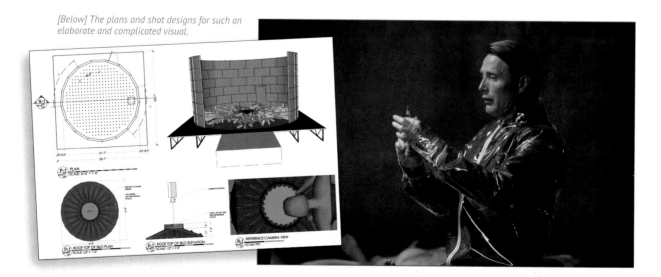

BEE MAN

Fans of the show will be happy to learn that people who work on the set of *Hannibal* are just as amazed by the exquisite grotesqueries that are the murder scenes.

"Those death tableaus are really, really spectacular," Fishburne says. "Our prosthetics team, they work miracles. I've seen them do some things where they've been operating in their workshop around the clock for four or five days straight where they've been up trying to create these beautiful terrors. I think Bee Man was the one that knocked me out of my socks."

"A lot of people like The Bee Man," Dagenais says.

Finding The Bee Man: Real bees were used for some of the shots and the crew were forced to don protective gear. Up close and inside the victim, however, the real bees were replaced by CG.

Given the trials endured to finish the piece, it's amazing that even the team that created it have affection for him.

Occasionally the road from concept to finished product is a bumpy one, whether the obstacles are technical challenges or, in the case of The Bee Man, miscommunication. In fact, the initial challenge for Dagenais in making this hero piece was not the grand scope or the fine details of constructing it, but a more cosmetic concern.

"We asked them to send us the actor they wanted this body to look like and we were going to make this body out of. They sent us a guy that was so hairy," he says, "that we could not cast him. So we moulded his head and then we asked them to send us someone else."

The original performer for the casting of the head was in his sixties but the replacement actor sent for the body work was closer to eighteen and a much rounder, softer body type.

[Below] Early production art for The Bee Man. Several avenues were explored while trying to find the right visual for the episode.

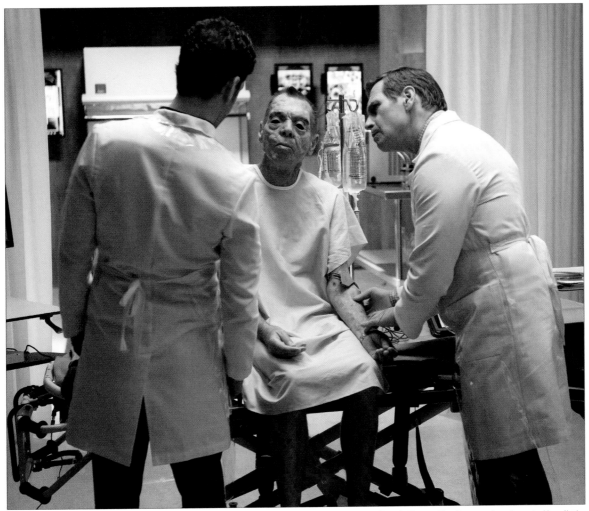

[Above] Katherine Pimms' (Amanda Plummer) second victim, still alive, provides a vital clue to Beverly Katz, taking her one step closer to Hannibal.

"We had a head and body that did not match," Dagenais says. "So that was a little bit of an issue."

Once it was complete, Dagenais and his team were satisfied with the results, despite the fact their artistic sensibility and technical acumen might have been discredited by a body that was comprised of the original actor's head and hand, the young man's torso and arms and somebody else's legs.

"It was a big mish-mosh of things," he says. "But the final product was fine, the final result was nice... I liked it.

"But sometimes it's bumpy getting there. And that was something that was out of our control," Dagenais noting that it wasn't the original actor's fault that he was more hirsute than previously encountered.

One can assume that the unexpected last-minute curve ball on a television series as demanding as *Hannibal* happens often. But is a smooth ride during the prosthetics process a rare occurrence?

"It's not rare," Dagenais says. "But more often than not there will be these sort of things that happen. It still can run smoothly with those little bumps...it's

when things go horribly wrong, and that happens once in a while, but hopefully not too often."

An even bigger issue than the Frankenstein body was the creation of the honeycombs, which Dagenais and his team thought they could replicate by moulding the contents of actual beehive containers.

"That was physically impossible to duplicate because it's so incredibly thin. So we sought out our own idea: How do you make your own? We ended up finding certain things where we could physically control the thickness of the walls of the honeycombs. We made a big plate of that, moulded it and ran sheets and sheets of beehive material and fabricated the stuff on the guy on the tree."

Anthony Patterson from Rocket Science VFX had to create the bees for the exterior shot of the body, noting that they "used real bees to shoot the element" but that the entire interior of The Bee Man "was replaced with CG bees and hives".

The result was one of the most quietly disturbing displays made for the show, one that put an emphasis on the vulnerability over the viscera of the victim.

THE TREE OF LIFE...
& DEATH

Although, where would we be without the viscera seen in the breathtaking beauty of the Grand Guignol scene known as The Tree of Life. It is hard to imagine a major network airing a series where a city councilman is pinned to a tree, vines twisting through his body like veins (or "varicose vines" as Brian Zeller puts it at the crime scene), and his chest split open and organs replaced with assortments of poisonous flowers. Considering the show's circumspection of the psychiatric discipline, is it too far to suggest a similar take on the politician, with lungs intact to confirm his "wind bag" status?

That Hannibal has consulted his recipe cards for Steak and Kidney Pie before the discovery of the councilman may explain why he has taken every organ from the politician except for his lungs. What that

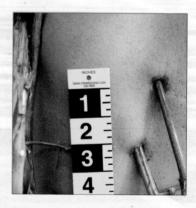

[Above] Crime scene photographs and close-ups of The Tree of Life.

recipe doesn't explain is the replacement of these organs with Bella Donna for the heart, a chain of White Oleander for the intestines, and Ragwort for the Liver.

Each flower is chosen with care. For example, the Bella Donna (also known as Deadly Nightshade) is severely toxic and contains hyoscyamine and scopolamine, both compounds known to cause the kind of hallucinations Dr. Lecter is known to generate for some of his patients. It is the kind of care and pride of handiwork that makes Jack Crawford nervous as he assesses the crime scene.

Would the show have quite the same impact if, for example, we weren't able to see the flowers arranged in the split-open councilman?

Looking at the work of The Tree of Life, it is easy to see that if it weren't for the explicit nature of the crimes, the audience wouldn't feel the same level of engagement with these high stakes.

Dagenais thinks that while the show is a well-made drama on its own, the messy business of murder is required, and not just to show the true effect of violence on those who are victimized by the act and the aftermath.

"What saves these guys," Dagenais says about the production, "is that they do show more but it's done well. It's not gore for the sake of it. It needs to be gory but not necessarily revolting. Everything is a nice piece to look at, as morbid as it can be. I think it wouldn't be the same if they *didn't* show that stuff."

[Below] The individual, poisonous flowers used in the gruesome tableau. Left to right: Bella Donna, white oleander, and ragwort. [Far right] The flowers in their bed.

WILL GRAHAM

HUGH DANCY

Will Graham

In a show full of mirrored relationships, none is more compelling than the central struggle between Hannibal and Will Graham. As with a reflective surface, the similarities are just as compelling as the differences.

At the start of the show, Graham has removed himself from active duty as a profiler and retreated to the world of teaching.

"I always assumed that it was because it was too much for him," actor Hugh Dancy says. "And he felt that the next most productive activity for him would be to train other people."

There is also a sense that while the act of profiling comes at a steep cost, Graham is also aware of his own attraction to that violent side of himself. And he's frightened of it.

"He's been holding it at arm's length, but once the door is opened for him again by Jack Crawford, he starts to go down that slope quite quickly."

Graham finds an unsuspecting—and certainly unorthodox—friend in Hannibal Lecter during this slippery slope. When Hugh Dancy discusses the relationship, he mentions how Graham has never been closer to another person than he is to Hannibal.

"In a sense, the two of them have been wandering the Earth, totally isolated, because they have such a specific and elevated mentality," he suggests. "Not identical, but it is as if not only are you the greatest chess player on the planet, you're actually the only person on the planet that can play chess. And then suddenly you walk into a room one day and there's a guy playing chess. I think that's how they feel about each other."

It's a complicated relationship, one muddied by the realization that one of them is a cannibalizing serial killer, but it's not a deal-breaker.

"It's a very rich and profound friendship, and love even," Dancy explains. "Once Will realizes who Hannibal is, it complicates that, but it doesn't just wipe the slate clean. It doesn't change the fact of their connection."

Further to the recognition of a kindred spirit is a similar linguistic facility and the ability to use it for full expressive intent.

"Hannibal can talk with the same level of profound insight as Will has about the acts of violent people, and that's reflected in the language. In the scenes that Will and Hannibal have when they're in Hannibal's office, when they're not directly therapizing Will and they're talking about the various different crimes, the language remains the same. It's very heightened, almost poetic, and full of imagery. That's not the case when Will talks to Jack about the crimes. Jack just wants answers. 'Just tell me who did it. What weapon did he use?'"

WOLFTRAP & THE DOGS

Will needs a place to hide and tend to his wounds. If Hannibal creates a "re-natured nature" to best express and contain his curated life, Will Graham relies on nature to provide a respite, and protection, from the horror of violence he witnesses every day on duty. So it follows that if Hannibal's house is as ornate as a Chinese box, then Graham's is plain as one designated for shoes.

"Sightlines were definitely a consideration," says Patti Podesta. Everyone agreed that a man as psychologically fragile and hyper-vigilant as Graham would want to be aware of anyone showing up outside. "It was David Slade's idea that he would sleep downstairs."

Podesta suggested that Graham would require a softer, rounded space; a sanctuary with the thinnest possible membrane between interior and exterior.

"We decided that Will purchased a farmhouse in the lands outside of Quantico and just moved in," Podesta continues. "I found a perfect, uninflected house outside of Toronto."

The main floor of the house had long and wide windows that allowed an undisturbed flow from the interior to the lush, green world outdoors.

"He lives there with his dogs and very little else."

As for the dogs, Graham seems incapable of letting a single stray pooch out of his caring and compassionate

embrace. This befits a man who has trouble cultivating relationships with human beings; there is safety in a life with dogs and not just because of the security they provide. But if Bryan Fuller shares an aesthetic affinity with Hannibal Lecter, he also can easily relate to Graham's affection for strays.

"Bryan loves dogs," Matthew Davies reports. "You'll rarely come across any animals suffering in his scripts."

When one of the dogs from Will Graham's pack was killed by a coyote on the farm where it lived outside of Toronto, he took it very much to heart.

"Bryan was beside himself...he was just devastated. He wanted to dedicate the episode to the dog that passed."

[Above] Will welcoming Winston, the newest member of the Graham pack. It is through Winston we see the tender, compassionate side of Will.

[Left] The floorplan for Will's house, including furniture placement and the location of the dog beds.

THE
MINNESOTA SHRIKE

There are many species of the shrike, and most are loners with a severe call. They belong to the *Laniidae* family, which derives its name from the Latin word for "butcher". Garret Jacob Hobbs' *nom de assassiner*, then, is well-earned.

Not only does this killer have a proclivity for eating his victims, he uses every bit of their bodies like a good hunter would.

More important to the series is not Hobbs' prodigious killing output so much as his death at the hand of Will Graham. Not only does it initiate him into the subterranean thrill of murder (including Hobbs' dying word to Graham: "See?"), but it also firmly establishes Graham as a man of great interest to the diabolical Lecter.

After Will kills the Minnesota Shrike, Lecter sees something in the bookish agent that catches his eye.

"He recognizes something that eventually can go down the same path as Hannibal," Mads Mikkelsen says. "It might take a couple of short-cuts—it's not going to be the exact same path as Hannibal's—

The cabin and preparation room [below] where Abigail helped her father dress his kills.

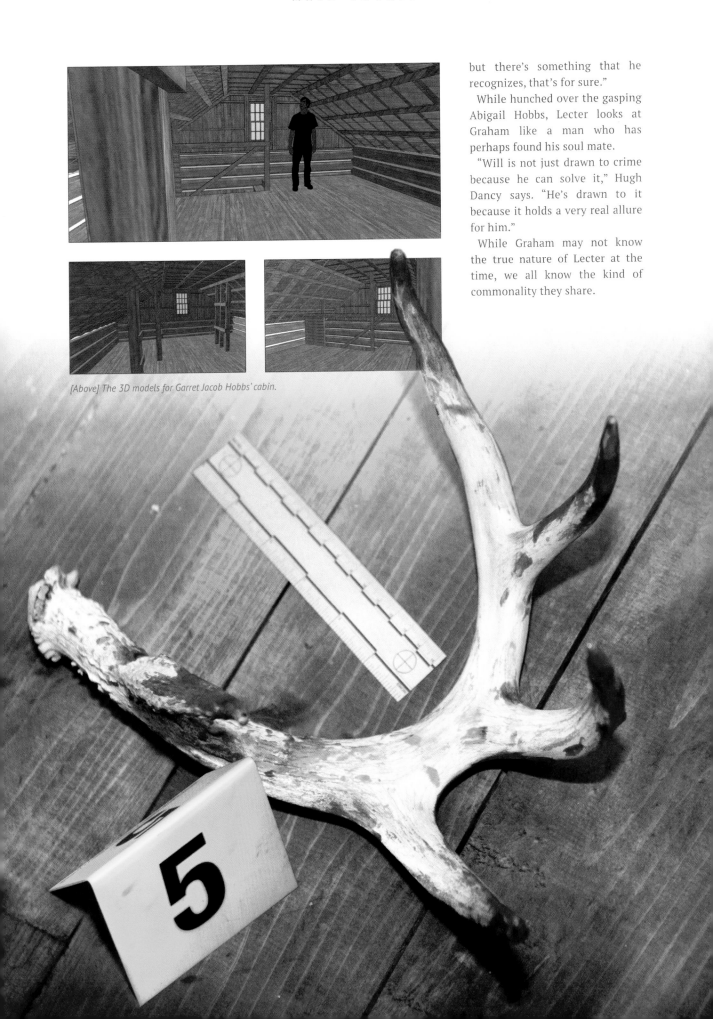

[Above] The 3D models for Garret Jacob Hobbs' cabin.

but there's something that he recognizes, that's for sure."

While hunched over the gasping Abigail Hobbs, Lecter looks at Graham like a man who has perhaps found his soul mate.

"Will is not just drawn to crime because he can solve it," Hugh Dancy says. "He's drawn to it because it holds a very real allure for him."

While Graham may not know the true nature of Lecter at the time, we all know the kind of commonality they share.

"Obviously we all know what Hannibal's got going on in his basement," Dancy says. The two also share a robust disdain for the majority of other human beings.

"Hannibal is more of a connoisseur," Dancy suggests. "I think he's found ways to take pleasure in people… Will is so protective of himself that he doesn't have the social outlets Hannibal has. But for both of them, most people are a bit of a painful experience."

Just as painful as the Shrike's propensity for mimicking his namesake, is his chosen form of trophy room: the attic stuffed to bursting with antlers.

"Talk about life imitating art or art imitating life," Matthew Davies says. "But these rooms do exist. A lot

of hunters do mount the horns on the walls and it does get to a point where it becomes this thorny bush."

Even eerier is the dream sequence when Garret Jacob Hobbs appears next to Graham as he puts the menacing stag in the crosshairs of his rifle. The "deer blind" they stand in is a small-scale replica of Graham's house and that is no poetic flourish.

"It was scripted that it would be a deer blind and suggested to the director, who took it to Bryan, that it should be a miniature of his own house," Davies says. "Which does exist…certain hunters will reproduce scaled versions of their own homes up in trees and on platforms to hunt deer from above."

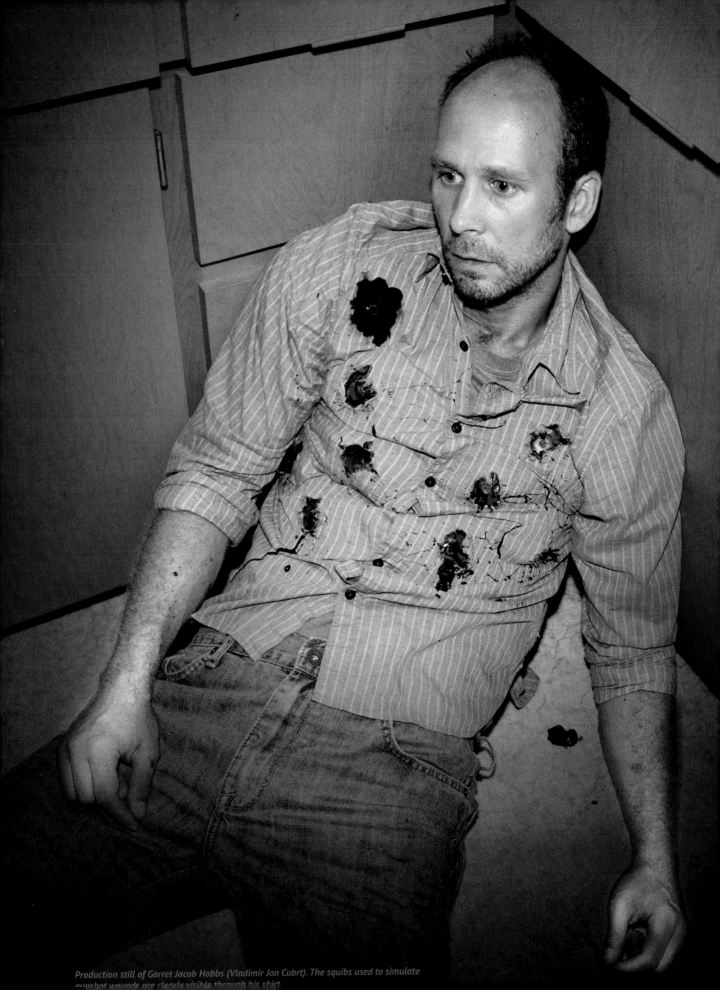

Production still of Garret Jacob Hobbs (Vladimir Jon Cubrt). The squibs used to simulate gunshot wounds are clearly visible through his shirt.

ABIGAIL HOBBS

The death of Garret Jacob Hobbs casts a long shadow across the show, especially in the first season. That falls in line with the prevailing attitude of how violence is handled in the series, and the long-term effect of both viewing and participating in a vicious exchange. The interesting aspect of the murder of Garret Jacob Hobbs is that while it unleashes a murderous riptide in Will Graham's character, it obliquely provides an opportunity for redemption.

The Talmudic notion that once you save a life you are responsible for it is certainly a consideration for Graham. But as with everything else in Hannibal, it is a situation that steps to its own uniquely logical drumbeat.

"For Will the issue is that he's gone into the Hobbs' house and killed someone for the first time," Hugh Dancy says. "In a sense he had to do it but, as he tells Hannibal, he actually enjoyed it. That has fired up the part of himself that he is very afraid of. Abigail represents the possibility for him to be a savior, to be more benevolent."

It is a lofty target for Graham, and one he no doubt embarks upon as a survival tactic following his foray into homicide: how better to counteract his newly awakened appetite for homicide than through the saving of a seemingly worthy, youthful soul? But the father surrogate mantle he assumes is quite problematic, given the late father's extra-curricular

[Right] Abigail (Kacey Rohl) recovering from her father's attack and [below] the 3D plans for her hospital room. The arrowed A - E's designate the camera angles used in the scene.

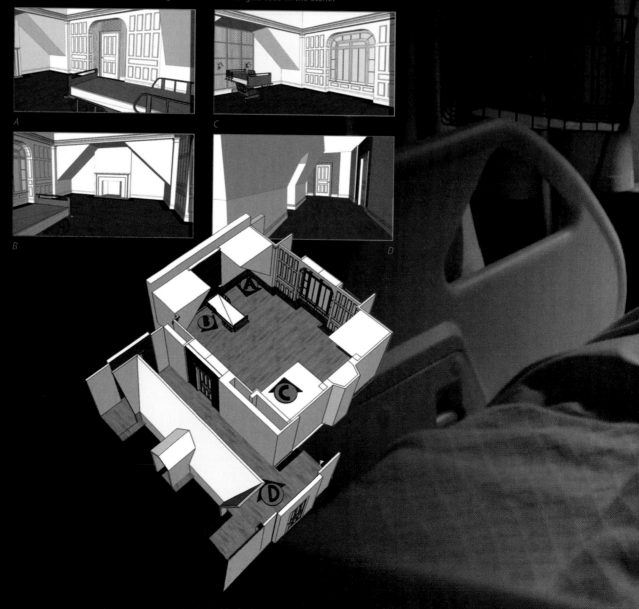

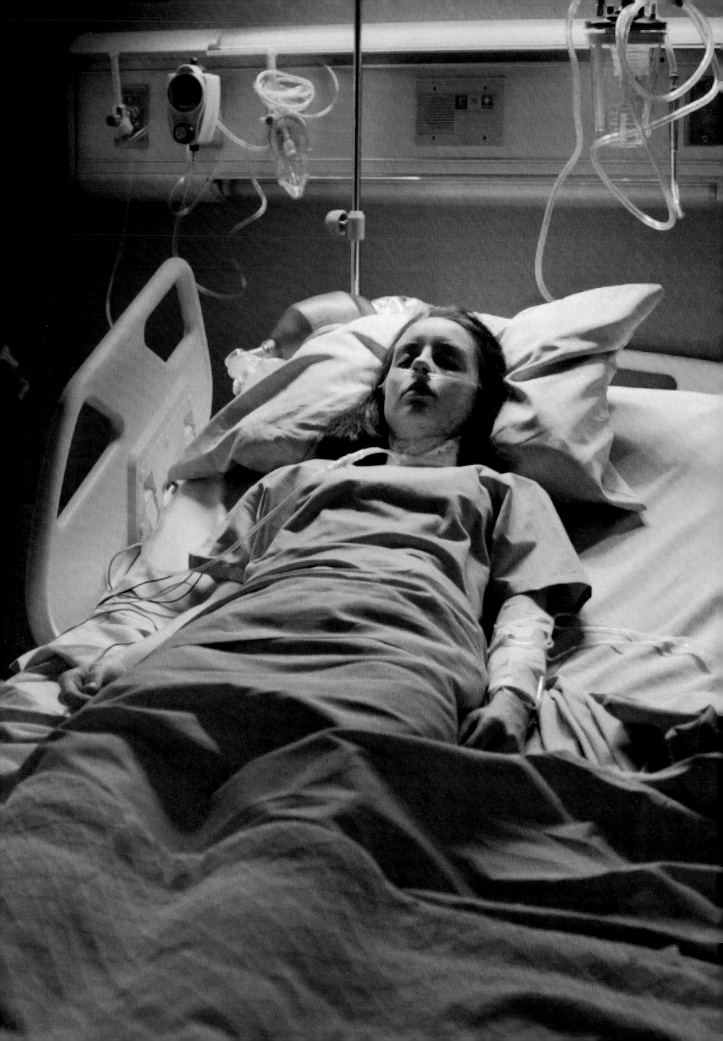

The sequence of events from Abigail's attack to waking up with the realization of her parents' fates.

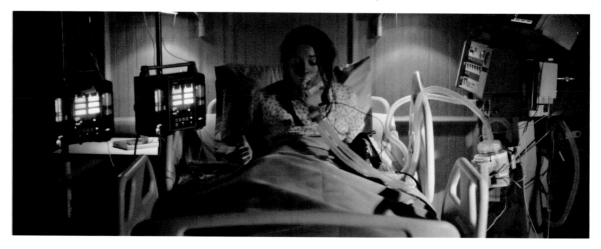

activities and abhorrent (to say nothing of implicative) inclusion of his daughter in that hobby.

"The problem is that by seeing himself as a father figure to Abigail he's also stepping more and more into the shoes of Garret Jacob Hobbs, who is a cannibal and serial killer. So it's a pretty messy family dynamic."

Messier still is the bridge that it erects between Graham and Hannibal. In a show that is full of dangerous mentor/protégé relationships (Will and Hannibal, Will and Jack Crawford, even Hannibal and Alana in both a romantic and culinary aspect), the one that Will enters into with Abigail is fraught with peril, and no less so for Hannibal's similar interest. The bloody scene at the Hobbs' home is what draws the two of them together, both in connection to Abigail and beyond.

"It's a complicated thing, clearly," Dancy says of the triad. "He does feel, in some way, responsible for Abigail, as does Hannibal."

The end of the pilot episode is a striking demonstration of that impulse in both men, not to mention an ambitious target to reach within the first chapter of the series.

"The final shot of that first episode with Hannibal and Will on either side of her in a kind of uncomfortable triptych, was a brilliant place to get to in one episode," Dancy says. "And it established what draws Will and Hannibal together, and our sense of responsibility, a

[Right] Set pieces for Abigail's hospital room.

kind of parental responsibility and love, for Abigail. And that gets explored all the way through the first two seasons."

The role of performance in establishing this bizarre triangle was critical. While the level of acting expertise and emotional intelligence brought to the set by Dancy and Mikkelsen is already established, none of what followed would have been possible if the Abigail leg of the triangle table was wobbly.

When discussing the actual amount of gore on screen versus the perception of it by the audience, director David Slade is quick to laud the actress who played

Abigail. In this performance, an actress was required to embody the essence of a young, perhaps even naïve, woman while managing to believably portray a complicit agent in her father's serial killings. It is a tall order for any actor to project innocence while luring other young women into the Shrike's beak.

"Kacey Rohl, who plays Abigail Hobbs, was so evocative," he says. "So able to personify a really base horror...I always felt that when you talk to people, and what they really responded to, you'd think 'Well, there was actually very little on screen at all.' You just thought there was something really horrible there."

[Below] Abigail takes a dark step into Hannibal's world in season one, episode three, but her reaction to and murder of Nicholas Boyle (Mark Rendall) intrigues Hannibal enough for him to take her firmly under his wing.

FISHING FOR MEMORIES

While locked away in the Baltimore Hospital for the Criminally Insane, Will Graham finds himself framed as a serial killer. He is alienated by his colleagues in the FBI and, most worryingly, kept from his place as alpha male to his dog pack at home.

Despite visits from Abigail and Jack Crawford, and his puppet-master machinations to have Hannibal Lecter murdered, Will still needs something to while away the long hours. A respite from the gloom of his cell and crumbling life.

What better than fantasies about fly-fishing?

"That's his one relief from this dark world, isn't it?" says Director of Photography James Hawkinson.

Those sequences, while drenched in sunlight, were still shot when the sun was very low on the horizon and harbour a bittersweet element: in a series where some of the most grotesque death tableaus occur away from the dark of night, even the light of day comes with complications.

"That kind of light," Hawkinson says, "it brings out nostalgia...and there's something melancholic about sunsets to me. It's like, darkness is coming I suppose. He's maybe out of the darkness for a minute but it still has a melancholic, although idyllic, feel to it."

Hawkinson enjoyed shooting Graham fly-fishing immensely, and feels that it was a necessary breather for the audience.

"It's important for an audience, for the human brain, to keep stimulated. To change it up and give them different imagery. But the thing about this show is that so much of the imagery is dream imagery and it works on a subconscious level with so many people. It's the kind of show you wake up from rather than watch."

THE MARLOW CASE

The startling homicide of the Marlow family that opens the entire series is not only a perfect introduction to the universe of *Hannibal*, but to the visual lexicon created to depict this world. The language of the show is specific and different, without the tropes of other crime procedurals to rest on. And for much of the show, the primary lens is that of Will Graham.

"The notion that we go through Will's imagination," David Slade recalls. "It was very, very clear to me how that should look and how that would work."

One of the most distinctive visual expressions of the show, and one seen from the very first episode, is the pendulum that arcs across the screen and removes things from a crime scene as Will enters his empathic state. While the notion was very specific from *Red Dragon*, Fuller latched onto what was expressed in a few sentences and expanded it into a series-defining trademark.

As for the director, Slade took time to determine the best way to visualize that process.

"It was a while before I figured out that it should be made of light so that it is part of the neural process... so it's not something solid, it's somewhat amorphous."

Once conceptualized, there remained the matter of producing it on screen.

"We did tons of testing trying various different things and it came down to Occam's razor," Slade recalls. "The simplest solution was put a light on a wire and swing it around."

Instead of employing CGI effects, Slade opted for the practical approach which allowed for highlights to travel along reflective surfaces on set and help give real-world weight to the flourish.

The Marlow crime scene is the first in which we see Will at work. Seeing our hero kill the victims while describing how, puts the viewer instantly on edge.

[Left] Scans of the documents Will leafs through to get to the details of how the killer gained access. All this paperwork was created accurately and faithfully to the real thing.

"I came up with that idea and it was a few weeks before I said, 'This is how we're going to do it.' On the day that we shot that first scene there would be a kino flo (fluorescent light) hanging from a wire and a guy on the ladder behind the camera swinging that left and right so you'd get these little highlights."

"Both Bryan and I are huge fans of practical make-up from movies like *The Thing*. *Salem's Lot* is a movie that comes up in conversation a lot as a childhood favourite."

The lesson learned from movies like those is "if you can do it in camera then it will look real."

We might learn another interesting lesson if we wonder why Will Graham would teach the unsolved murders of Mr. and Mrs. Marlow to his students of behavioural science. If we consider the timeline—that the opening murder takes place before Graham walked away from field work with the FBI—then we might surmise that his inability to find the killer could have played a role in his decision to retreat into teaching. And yet he can't let go of the case, revisiting the scene via his shocking in-class slideshow.

This reluctant tenacity might have been just the hint Crawford needed to believe that Graham still had a taste to try solving the unsolvable.

MUSHROOMS

Eldon Stammets, the pharmacist with the interest in cultivating fungi, provided an early taste of the morbid homicidal flourishes we would become accustomed to seeing in the continuing arc of *Hannibal*.

Appearing in the second episode of season one ("Amuse-Bouche"), the collection of bodies crossed with a mushroom garden proved not only a gasp for the audience but also provided the prosthetics team at Mindwarp Productions with a formidable task that would set the stage for requests to come.

"Time was an issue," François Dagenais says. "It was an earlier one so it was a little daunting because we hadn't hit our groove yet."

The initial concern was deciding what type of mushrooms would be used, both in the practical prosthetics but in the time-lapse required for Will

Graham's empathic rewind of the murder scene.

"From the point-of-view of us making mushrooms, we had to use mushrooms that we could mold and reproduce," Dagenais says. "We tried to sculpt some...but the ease of molding real things is always better."

Once the type of mushrooms was decided and Dagenais' team started running them on their assembly line, they had to approach the victims. They had bodies in stock so they went to work making them look as though they were in various stages of decomposition and then applying the moulded mushrooms.

While dressing the bodies for the set, Dagenais had the dreadfully ingenious idea that, when the tape is peeled back from the mouth of one of the pharmacist's prey, that his lips would come away as well (above). It helped to have an actor to work with on this gag, as he is the one who grabs Will's hand to indicate that he is still alive.

"We ended up making dentures that fit over his mouth and did a make-up," Dagenais recalls.

As for the time lapse, Rocket Science VFX came in when stock footage proved unsatisfactory. "We did these CG mushrooms in reverse time-lapsing," Robert Crowther says. "And that, to me, has a nice feeling of time rewinding."

PRAYING ANGELS

Perhaps some of the most dramatic murder scenes are the ones committed and dressed in "Coquilles" (season one, episode five). While other homicides investigated by Jack Crawford's Behavioral Science Unit also feature the theme of transformation, few have as grand Biblical connotations as the praying angels, killed and positioned into a penitent tableau by the avenging Elliot Buddish.

The uneasy partnership between murder and righteousness (as Buddish only kills those he thinks are deserving of death and in need of God's forgiveness) is not all that different than what used to be the case between practical prosthetic makers and designers of CG effects.

"It's not like it used to be," Dagenais reports. "'Oh my God, they're going to take over our job.' Now, sometimes we seek their help, sometimes they seek ours. It's a good work relationship."

For example, the prosthetic team might rely on visual effects to help simplify a stunt. "Instead of doing a huge make-up to hide a bloodline, stuck through the face for a nosebleed, they can erase that. Or they could erase a cut happening... we put on a cut and they erase it and let it show up again as the knife goes down."

In this case, it was a planned collaboration to adhere to budgetary constraints without sacrificing the impact of the praying angels.

"That was planned out," Robert Crowther from Rocket Science VFX says. "Part of it has to be done by the prosthetics department but it was our design. [We know] if we shoot these pieces, then we can put them together to create the look of the angel wings."

"It was very painterly," director of photography James Hawkinson says. "It had a very Caravaggio feel to it, how the light came into that room. It reminded me of Caravaggio's *Annunciation*, of Gabriel visiting

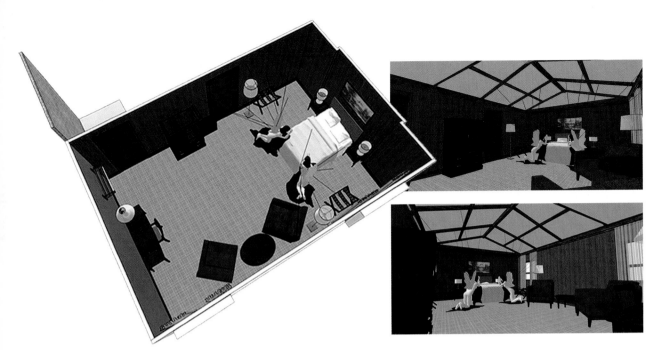

the Madonna. A lot of those death scenes...they're very artful, and evocative of a lot of different art work."

For those wondering how such a grim scene, complete with flayed skin serving as wings and the resultant exposed spines, might get past TV censors, it wasn't easy. But not, perhaps, for the reason you might think.

The production braced for word from Standards and Practices, and discovered that there was concern for the scene—however, it was for the nudity of the murder victims and not the gruesome defilement of their remains. Specifically, they were concerned about the blatant buttocks cleavage on display.

Even more telling than the shock of nudity over violence is how the problem was solved—more blood was added around the offending butt cracks and the episode went merrily to air.

[Below & Left] A hallucinatory side-effect of Elliot Buddish's (Seann Gallagher) brain tumor was the ability to see a person's sins. Elliot, the Angel Maker, believed he was saving his victims and ultimately himself.

THE JUDGE

When reviewing the work of Will Graham's admirer in dispatching Judge Davies, Hannibal makes note of the removed heart and brain placed on the scales and says,

"Justice is mindless and heartless."

Considering the genuine innocence of Graham in the murders attributed to him, we could easily say that, with the murder of Judge Davies and the inevitable mistrial, justice is triumphant in any action that acquits Will of these crimes.

The courtroom set was a previously existing one but the production design team went about refitting it to suit the needs of *Hannibal*, setting it apart from standard TV courtrooms. Not only does the space have greater texture in the contrast of warm timber and cool stone, but daylight bleeds in from the windows above the jury with the antiseptic sting of sunlight.

"We built this entire corridor and elevators and we made it twice as large and changed all the finishes and colours," production designer Matthew Davies recalls.

"I did huge classical paintings at both ends of the corridor and above the judge. A lot of the art work around Hannibal's office relates to Greek mythology and stories around cannibalism and, again, shows the depth of his education and background.

"All of the paintings have lateral references to the show."

None looms larger than the work that hangs behind the Judge, a detail from *The Triumph of Justice* by Dutch master Gabriël Metsu (below). The section of that painting reproduced for the show displays an overwhelmingly allegorical scene, with the figure of a single bare-breasted Justice defeating a supine and deceitful figure in the form of Avarice.

There are critics who submit that the painting was an overreach by the artist, produced by a man trying to create a work on a scale larger than previously attempted. It offers a tidy mirror for the work by the killer himself, whose staging of the Judge's body could be seen as the work of an enthusiastic amateur, and one armed with sledgehammer subtlety.

The creation of this set piece was initially to hinge on just as dramatic a staging—the director wanted to hang the real actor from the courtroom rafters.

"We were going to provide a little prosthetic and they were going to use a green cap on his head," François Dagenais recollects. "And then the more they were compromising because he had to be suspended a certain way, the more they got into the reality of keeping an actor in a harness all day. So at the last minute they asked, 'What can we do?'"

The actor was already on set so Dagenais cast his head and started constructing the body.

"We made some hands, made a head, we showed up

[Right] Early concept art for the Judge's murder tableau. The art department went through several concepts before creating the scene for the show.

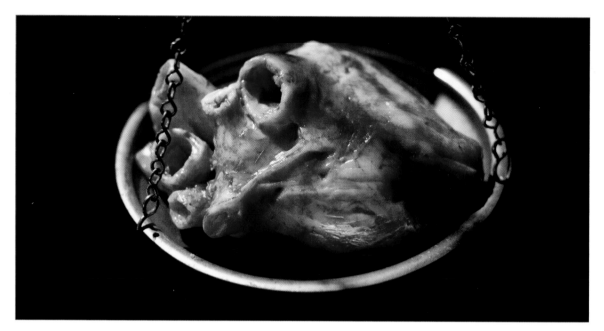

on set and they were happy because they didn't have to deal with someone suspended all day. The Judge was done in about two days."

The macabre nature of his work often gives Dagenais the chills. Many people think that it must weigh heavily on the mind of the man who engineers these nightmarish terrors, but they'd be surprised.

"Everybody asks me," Dagenais says, "'do you get nightmares making horrible things?' And I say, 'No. The only nightmares I have are to do with deadlines. How can we do *this* in *that* amount of time?' *That* gives me nightmares."

In the end, Dagenais is sanguine about the pressures he and his team are under. "It's always the final product, right? It doesn't really matter how you get there as long as what you give them is what they want and looks good."

Speaking of looking good, when Hannibal takes his seat on the witness stand, Will has a vision of him as the Wendigo Man. It is a chilling sight that is somehow made all the more creepy due to the fact that he wears the same suit as Hannibal and adopts his mannerisms.

Robert Crowther from Rocket Science VFX worked on this unnerving apparition by altering an actor who appeared on set in a Wendigo costume.

"We thin his neck, we thin his arms," Crowther says. "There are natural seams in the costume that we remove... we give him more of a ribcage and a gaunt body." This gives the Wendigo its mythical half-man, half-monster appearance. Deeply associated with cannibalism and psychosis, Will's hallucination of Hannibal as the Wendigo is not only visually unsettling, but becomes a portent to Hannibal's true nature.

[Above & Below] Close-ups on Mindwarp FX's prosthetic work on the Judge's head and heart. The Judge's murder is central to the season arc in that it, indirectly, acquits Will. [Right] The camera rig and team shooting the iconic scene. Left to right: Patrick King ("A" Dolly Grip), Pete Sweeney ("A" Camera Operator) and Barrett Axford ("A" Camera First Assistant).

BALTIMORE HOSPITAL FOR THE CRIMINALLY INSANE

Those familiar with the world of Thomas Harris will understand the themes of distrust in the foundations of psychiatry and those who practice it. How could it be any other way with a central practitioner of the art who makes an equal art of devouring human beings?

"Every psychiatrist in the show is damaged and not to be trusted," Patti Podesta wisely points out. "There is an explicit text throughout, in both the writing and the design, warning of the institutional power of psychiatry."

Not only does Matthew Davies note that Bryan Fuller creates the show with a "particular Gothic hybrid" but that his department also goes to "great lengths to prevent locations and smaller incidental sets that exist as narrative catalysts from being banal."

Nowhere is this more barefaced than in the Baltimore State Hospital for the Criminally Insane. A psychological hall of mirrors that is a hybrid of Gothic and Brutalist inclinations (and perhaps with inspiration from Carlo Scarpa's design for the Castelvecchio Museum in Verona), the design of the panopticon-style space was created not only as a "narrative catalyst" but with the shooting style of director of photography James Hawkinson in mind.

"He likes duller surfaces," Davies says. "He likes control of the reflections on the sets. He likes the opportunity to light from above...that requires removable ceiling pieces. He likes tonally very dark walls."

But if the surroundings are full of decaying metal bars and God's eye vantage points, then what of the man who runs it?

FREDERICK CHILTON & WILL

Like Panoptes from Greek mythology (the finest watchman due to his one hundred eyes), Dr. Frederick Chilton sees and hears all that goes on in his hospital. Unfortunately, Chilton has neither the circumspection nor the wit to see fully the dangers before him.

"Bryan is having a mighty good time punching that character over and over again," Caroline Dhavernas says. "And Chilton always comes back. Of all the characters, Chilton is the more *Twin Peaks*-ish."

Chilton is played by Broadway star Raúl Esparza,

known for singular performances in productions of *Speed-the-Plow, Taboo, Chitty Chitty Bang Bang,* Pinter's *The Homecoming* and Stoppard's *Arcadia,* along the way earning the distinction of being nominated in all Tony Award categories available to a male performer without a win.

"He's the craziest one," Dhavernas continues. "And I love how Raúl is having fun with it and bringing it to a whole new level."

No less unprincipled than the Dr. Chilton that appears in the books, the incarnation by Esparza brings preening

changes to the character, one who is quite convinced of his own greatness as a psychiatrist. Even when he thinks that his ethically dubious acts might result in the end of his career, he is less concerned for the fate of his patients as he is for his own reputation, a sure sign of a man in the business of healing minds for all the wrong reasons.

Hugh Dancy goes further, suggesting that Chilton is not only a bad psychiatrist but that he is a duplicitous man who has no right being in charge of so many fragile, devious minds.

"Will feels disdain for Chilton on a lot of different levels," Dancy says. "As soon as I walk into Chilton's office, his antennae go up and he sees a golden opportunity for advancement. When that doesn't work out then he wants to have me in his cells to study me in a different way."

When things start to go catastrophically wrong for Chilton, it is hard not to feel somewhat sorry for him, but in a way that is usually reserved for a bully who finally picks a fight with a much stronger opponent.

"At a certain point it's hard to believe he still deserves what's coming to him. But, at the same time, he walked into the lion's den. Initially, Chilton just aggravates Will and doesn't want to have anything to do with him, but by the time Will's in the asylum he starts to actively enjoy batting him around with his paw."

[Below] Dr. Chilton's (Raúl Esparza) fate. Drugged by Hannibal, he wakes in season two, episode seven, to discover two mutilated FBI agents in his home.

ABEL GIDEON

One of Chilton's sins is the "psychological driving" that allows Dr. Abel Gideon to believe that he is actually The Chesapeake Ripper, and not just a man responsible for the murder of his wife and her family along with a Baltimore State Hospital nurse. Gideon afforded Fuller the prospect to continue his reinvention of the world and the expectations of the audience.

"The opportunity to reinvent *The Silence of the Lambs* and Anthony Hopkins' interpretation of the character," Fuller says, was neatly balanced by the appearance of Gideon.

"Since we had so departed with that with Mads Mikkelsen's interpretation, it was fun to provide the audience and ourselves with a bit of juxtaposition with what [Gideon] represents as a sort of pretender to the throne and also as a psychopath in his own right."

Gideon is a character possessed of a mordant sense of humour and with the casting of such a giant in the comedy world, one could be left to wonder how much of that aspect of Abel was on paper and how much Eddie Izzard brought to the set.

"It is primarily buoyed by Eddie's talent in the role and in life," Fuller admits. "I think Eddie is one of the great minds of our generation. I think of him less as a comedian and more of a philosopher."

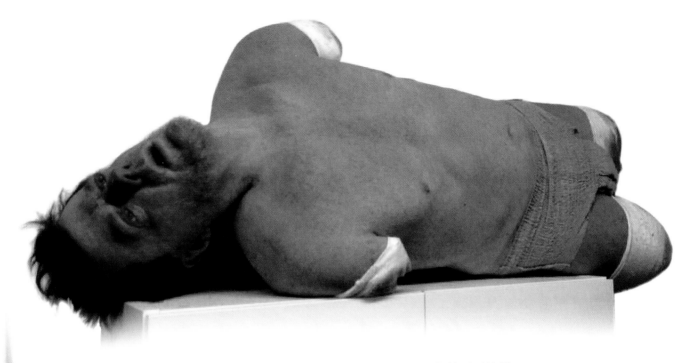

[Above] The full body prosthetic of the remains of Abel Gideon (Eddie Izzard) after Hannibal has had his fill.

First known to British audiences as the incisive stand-up comedian who appeared on stage in drag, Izzard quickly became just as well-known for his dramatic turns in TV roles such as *The Riches, United States of Tara* and *The Good Wife.* After working with Izzard in the proposed *The Munsters* remake *Mockingbird Lane,* Fuller knew that he wanted to work with the actor again.

There are many reasons to consider the right actor for such a role: he was the unwitting victim of insidious psychological manipulations that have comprised his own awareness of who he is, believing Chilton regarding his identity as The Chesapeake Ripper. When this delusion cracks, Gideon doesn't retire to a plush institution to engage in rigorous therapy to correct his personality schism, he embarks on a war path for revenge.

"So within all of those elements, there is an absurdity of a situation that I think you need someone as facile as Eddie Izzard to navigate in order to maximize the fun in the role."

THE WOUNDED NURSE

The history behind the inspiration for Abel Gideon's presentation of the nurse he kills reaches back to the sixteenth century but also has resonance with the canon relationship between Will Graham and Hannibal Lecter.

Originally appearing in *Feldbunch der Wundarzney* (Field Book of Surgery), the Wounded Man woodcut by Hans Wechtlin was meant to instruct surgeons on all manner of battlefield injuries, from cannonball trauma to bone-setting and treatment of injuries from sword play. First published in 1517 (with text written by Hans von Gersdorff and based on the writings of medieval surgeon Guy de Chauliac), the book also included directions on the amputation of limbs, a procedure von Gersdorff was rumoured to have completed over 200 times.

Of course in *Red Dragon*, Graham is tipped off to Lecter's true identity as The Chesapeake Ripper by the appearance of The Wounded Man drawing in his office, a trope repurposed in the series for the unfortunate Miriam Lass, who suffered a more lasting punishment for seeing past Lecter's carefully constructed veil.

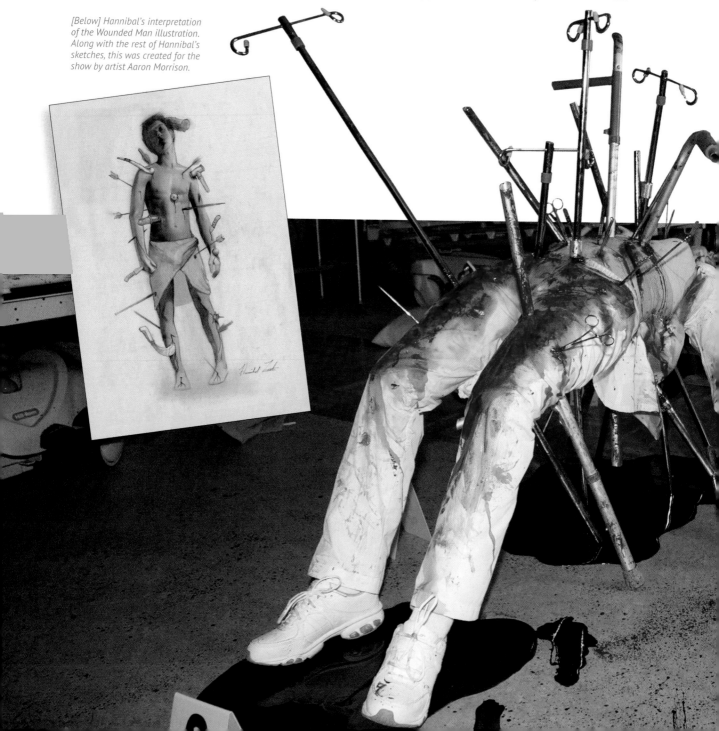

[Below] Hannibal's interpretation of the Wounded Man illustration. Along with the rest of Hannibal's sketches, this was created for the show by artist Aaron Morrison.

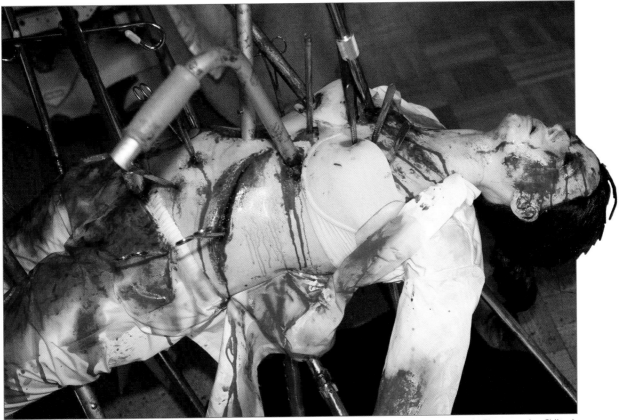

[Above & Below] Gideon's murder tableau crime scene of his nurse (season one, episode six) in the style of the Chesapeake Ripper, proving Chilton's 'driving' has convinced Gideon he is someone he is not.

THE OBSERVATORY

When Abel Gideon breaks out of confinement and starts to target the psychiatrists who dared to help him, he leaves most of them dead and caught in the freeze-frame writhing of The Columbian Necktie. Given the elective surgery Gideon has in mind, Chilton might have thought that the fate of the other doctors was preferable.

The motivation for Gideon's handiwork—other than taking the slimy Chilton to task for his psychological driving—is to flush out the real Chesapeake Ripper. He hopes to do this by selecting a number of Chilton's organs for removal and arranging them in a "gift basket" of surgical trophies.

That Gideon chooses to do so while Chilton is under local anaesthetic is a horrifying notion (despite the attending surgeon's insistence that this is the best manner in which to operate, to remind himself that he has a person's life in his hands). It is interesting that such a creative use of anatomical knowledge results in one of the less strenuous special effects scenes—the belly incision and retractor used are standard issue in any medical procedural drama. But the idea of finding out how many organs the body can "offer up before it truly begins to suffer" is the sort of theoretical experiment that one assumes Hannibal Lecter could put his full weight behind,

[Below] Director Guillermo Navarro, beside the camera, on set for season one, episode eleven.

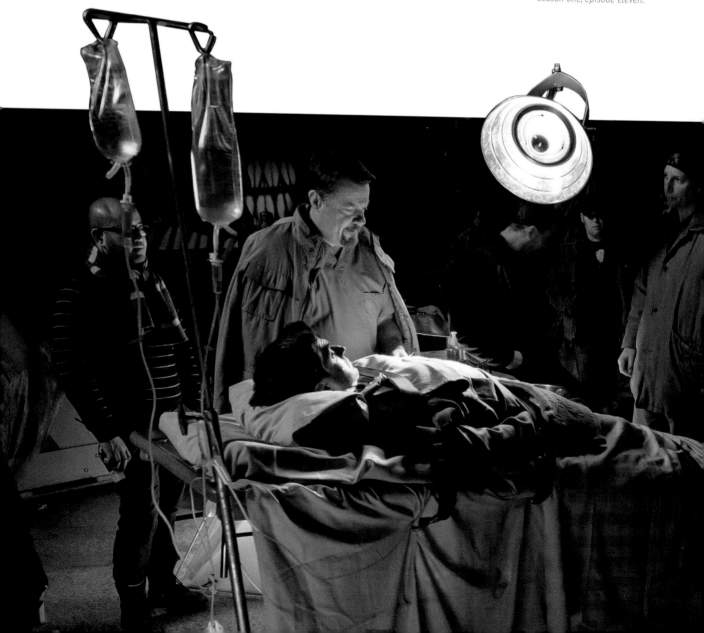

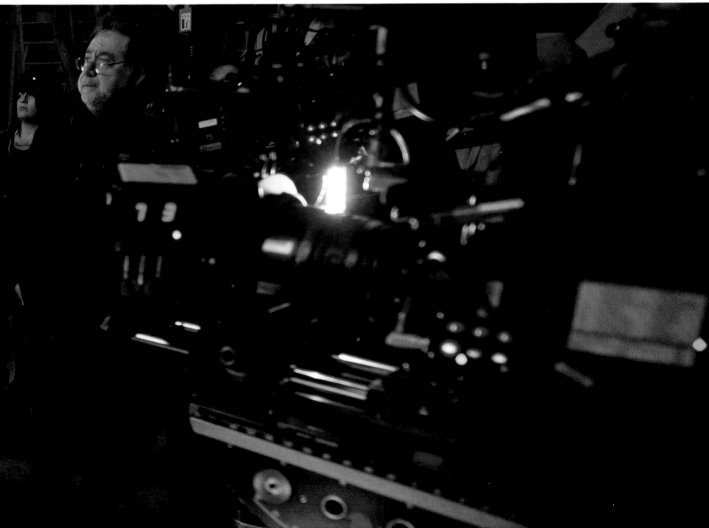

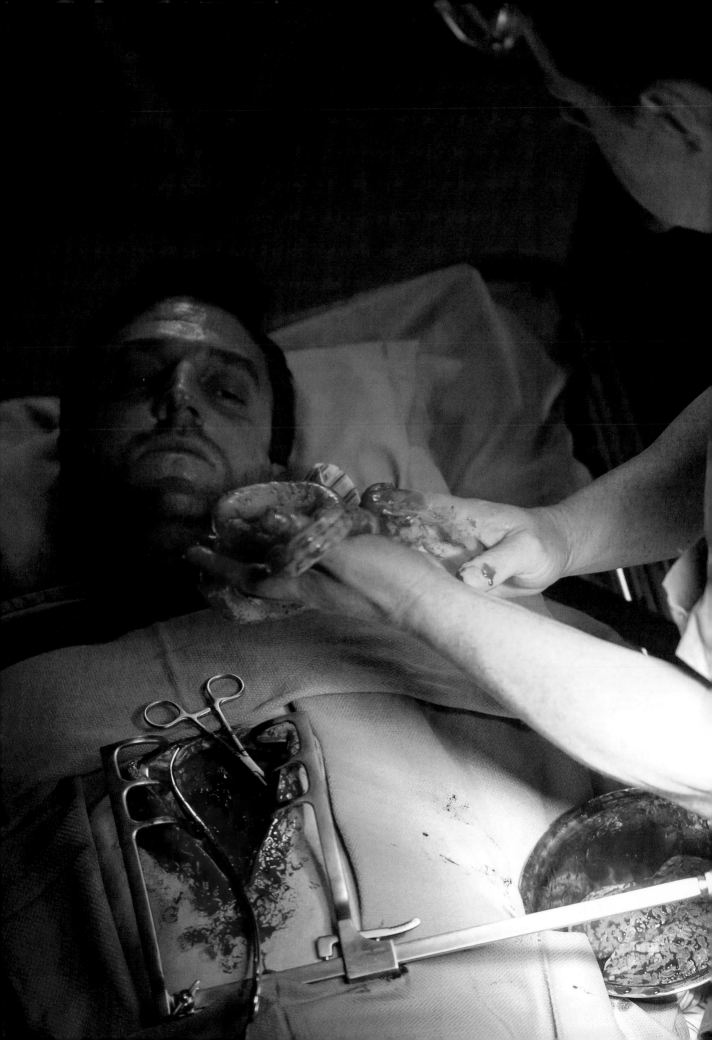

even if only for the rosy culinary specimens the work yields.

Such strategic thought experiments became the marching orders for this episode as Fuller and his writing staff found out after finishing the episode that Raúl Esparza and Eddie Izzard were only available for two days shooting. A Sunday night re-breaking of the script for shooting the following Thursday proved a strenuous task, especially when the writing room realized that they would need both actors together for at least one long day of shooting. The on-the-fly rewrite of the episode proved a challenge for everybody involved and even Fuller himself said that he is amazed the episode makes any sense at all given the last-minute turmoil.

[Left] Close-up on the gory detail of Gideon's evisceration of Dr. Chilton in season one, episode eleven.

[Below] Gideon wanted to leave a very clear message to Jack Crawford and the FBI using Freddie Lounds as a mouthpiece to detail Chilton's unethical, dangerous methods.

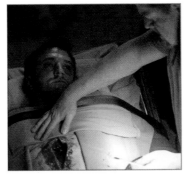

SORBET

DISSECTION OF A MURDER SCENE

TOTEM

[Above] Storyboard depicting the shots and camera angles of the discovery of the totem pole.

When the totem pole is discovered on a frozen beach, it is not easy for Crawford's team to find anything that links the victims. The methods of murder vary and there are very few links from one victim to the next. But the assemblage of these bodies, killed at varying times and in different stages of decomposition, is orchestrated by the hand of a deliberate and determined madman. More worrying is the "normalcy" by which Laurence Wells (played by genre stalwart Lance Henriksen, from film's *Aliens* to TV's *Millennium*) passes in society over the course of his slow-motion murder spree spread over forty years, and the legacy he hopes will survive his own time on Earth.

Fuller contends that the resignation with which Wells accepts his capture by the FBI, is not the result of a normal man paying the ultimate price for a domino effect set into motion by one misstep early in his life that lead to a trail of unmarked graves.

"I would argue that with Laurence Wells, he didn't think those were wrong decisions."

Fuller contends that he acted out very early in his

Joel Summers is the only recent victim. The others appear to be years, maybe decades, old. Exposure of graves suggests narcissism and desire for the world to see the killer's body of work.

Summers held particular significance. He is the key!

Joel Summers: Victim number 17.
Cause of death single stab wound to the heart.
Age: 40. Missing for 3 days.

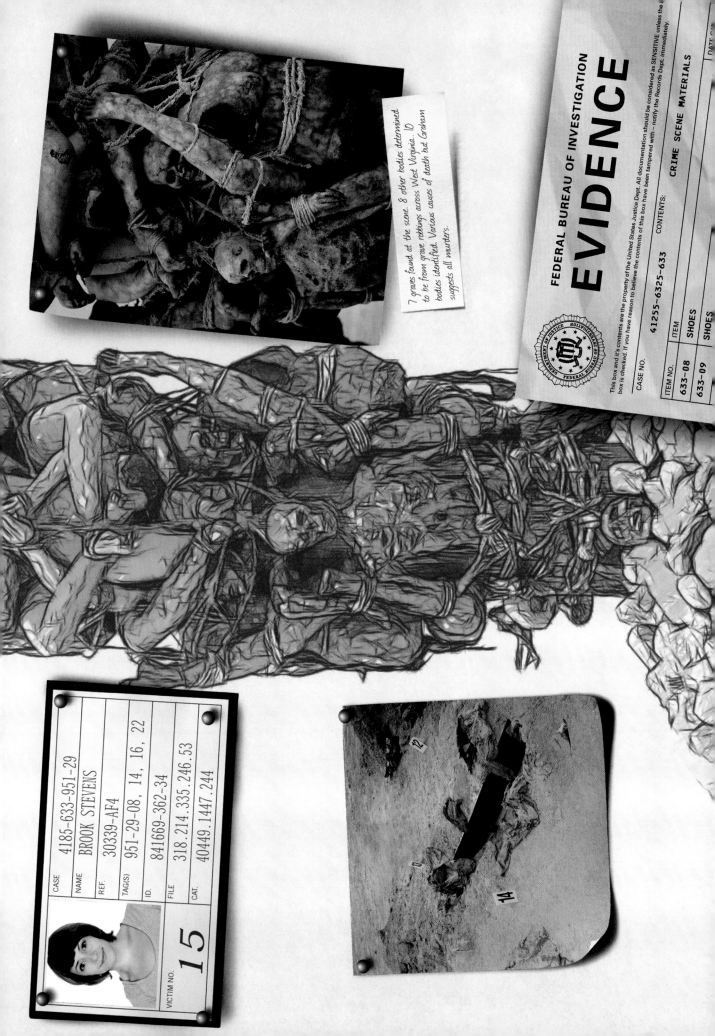

7 graves found at the scene. 8 other bodies determined to be from grave robbings across West Virginia. 10 bodies identified. Various causes of death but Graham suggests all murders.

CASE	4185-633-951-29
NAME	BROOK STEVENS
REF.	30339-AF4
TAG(S)	951-29-08, 14, 16, 22
ID.	841669-362-34
FILE	318.214.335.246.53
CAT.	40449.1447.244

VICTIM NO. 15

life and committed murder and, as reported by men who engage in the act, derived immense power and satisfaction from it.

"So he just did it quietly to feed his addiction."

Wells discovered that he was quite good at it, being so sanguine as to commit the murders differently each time so as not to establish a pattern.

"'And now that I'm of retirement age...pretty soon I'm not going to be able to take care of myself,'" Fuller posits in place of Wells. "'I'm going to find the most appropriate retirement package for someone in my position.' And that's jail."

While many of the killers on *Hannibal* are motivated to murder out of twisted sense of passion, Wells is colder with a more insidious quality. He was an undetectable malevolent force who then came out into the world like a cannonball in a mud puddle, with great pride in what he has accomplished.

"The irony of that is it all started with being in love with another woman," says Fuller. "A woman who had a child with another man and, realizing that after he had killed that other man and that other child eventually, that the child was indeed his own. So his life legacy about being a murderer could have been a life legacy about having a son and child and someone to carry on beyond his life."

The creation of the human totem pole could be looked at as just as much of a legacy-defining monument for François Dagenais and his team. Much of their work is a balance between the fantastical aims of each script and the creation and application of each piece on the day of shooting.

"They come up with something on paper," Dagenais says. "For us, we need to make sure that this doesn't fall apart...it has to stay together for the trip, it has to stay together while they shoot, and it has to be able to come apart for the next scene because it comes in [to the morgue] in pieces later on. So there's all these things we need to incorporate."

But beyond the practicalities of making a television series, the piece has to serve the story.

"There's a certain amount of realism that you need to keep...'How would he [Wells] have done that?'"

Just screwing body parts to a pole via fifteen-foot spinal cord of rebar may work for building and transportation, but it can have a negative impact on the story.

The first bridge to cross was deciding upon how the whole piece would actually look—it's easy to write "human totem pole" in a script, but what final form that takes is a process.

"They had an artist do a few renditions and eventually it got down to what it was," Dagenais says. "Now we take over."

At this point, they need to know what kind of detail will be required for filming.

"'Do you want to see a dressed stump on all of them? Does it need to be camera-ready in case you go right in?'"

In the end, they picked certain focal points on the totem pole, or "hero pieces", which were detailed enough for close-ups, and then made the rest as believable as possible without as much fine work as the "star" segments. "It's a balance between the minimum amount of work and the maximum amount of work," Dagenais says. "We ran body parts for days and then two days before it was due on set, we started putting stuff together."

They constructed the totem pole as per the production team's notes—rotten bodies on the bottom and fresher ones further up. For the final crowning piece on the pole, they had to build a whole body for the most recent kill, but one that would work just as well on top of the pole and on the autopsy table back at the FBI morgue.

The result is one of the most macabre crime scenes we've seen on television. It also made for a ghoulish commute for unsuspecting drivers—Dagenais and his team had to deliver the totem pole in pieces on the back of pick-up truck from a Toronto suburb to the set. Imagine driving your way into work and seeing stacked and rotting bodies on a flatbed.

Better eye-opener than a cup of coffee, wouldn't you say?

[Below & Right] The puzzle pieces of the human totem pole as created by François Dagenais and his team at Mindwarp FX. Some were aged to look decades old, some were still fresh and bloody.

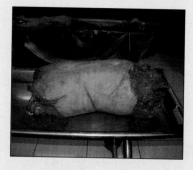

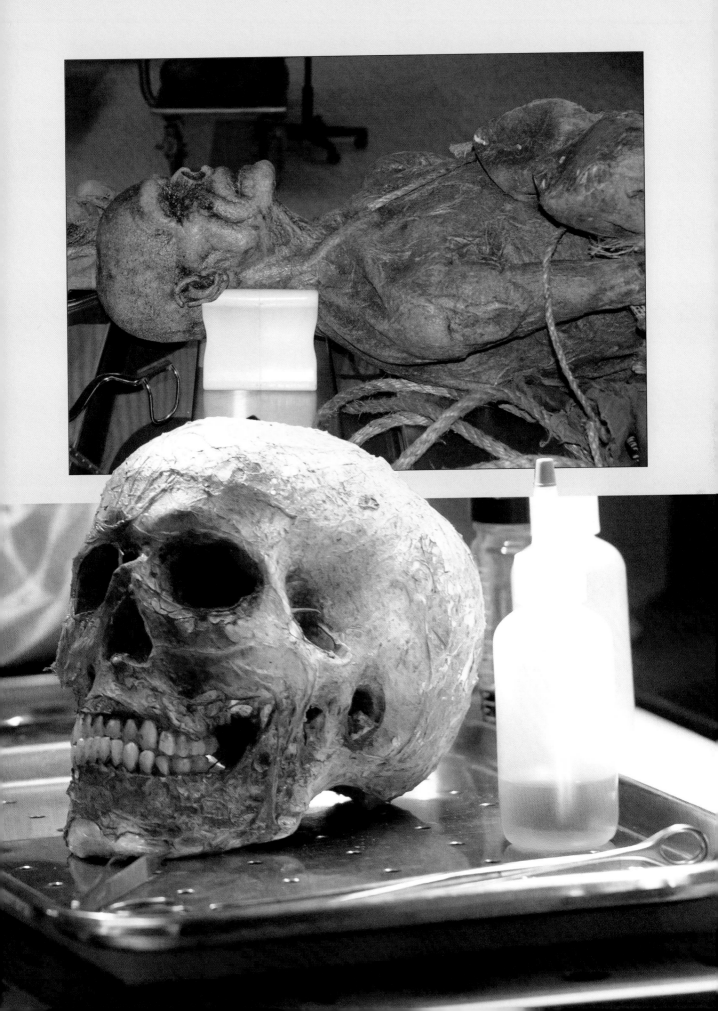

DESSERT
FINISHING TOUCHES

Editing and music are equally important facets of the filmmaking process and either can be as flashy or as subtle as required. In the case of *Hannibal*, there is more emphasis placed on the evocation of mood than directing the audience specifically how to feel.

Each episode of the show builds a somber, "slow burn" atmosphere and this is clearly the aim of Bryan Fuller, the respective directors, and the three editors who work on these episodes.

"I think there are many elements that create a sombre mood in *Hannibal*," says editor Ben Wilkinson. "Much of it is the pacing of the scenes. Because there is so much subtext and innuendo in the writing, we tend to let the words hang for a moment, allowing the dialogue to sink in during reactions. Quite often it is not what is said,

but what is not said. It's one of the things I love so much about this show, it isn't always in a hurry to fly through the scene."

Editor Michael Doherty concurs.

"At times we deliberately add air to some of the performances to help create the 'slow burn'. Also, we are not afraid to let shots linger, the antithesis of what you see on most television shows."

Stephen Philipson, editor, wrings as much suspense out of a situation as he can with this use of mood.

"Rather than cutting directly to a scary reveal," Philipson says. "I like to draw out the moment before the scare, to allow the audience to live in the dread and anticipation of what's to come. I also tend to show full camera moves from start to finish, to preserve their

elegance and impact, even if it slows down the pace. Thanks to the show's exceptional camerawork and bold visual design, we can hold on a shot to establish atmosphere without losing audience interest—we don't always have to cut to the chase!"

Cutting to the chase doesn't seem like an issue when it comes to the gore in the series, but there have been points where the editor's knife is required to make a scene a little more palatable.

Philipson says that, generally speaking, the network has been quite lenient with showing carnage.

"But there have been a few particularly violent shots deemed too upsetting."

The Violin Man created by Tobias Budge presented a challenge.

"We could show a tableau of the corpse after the conversion," Philipson says. "And abstract, non-specific shots of the conversion itself, but a close-up shot of the cello fret board being inserted in the man's throat did not pass."

Doherty exhibited similar restraint in the first season during the scene where Will Graham re-enacts Abel Gideon's murder of a nurse.

"We had a shot of Will's fingers pushing through the nurse's eyes. We played the scene more on Will's face and less on the nurse."

He also recalls an angle on Dr. Sutcliffe's Glasgow Smile that was "a lovely side shot...that was too horrific, even by Hannibal standards."

Ben Wilkinson also remembers when he toned down the cutting of a cheek in season two and a dream sequence where Graham imagines slitting Hannibal's throat while suspended over Mason Verger's pigs.

But it doesn't always break in favour of reducing the on-screen onslaught. One example is the Praying Angels from the first season.

"I remember thinking while cutting...that there is no way this will end up in the final cut. It did. I am still amazed by the amount of gore we were allowed to keep in, given this is a network show."

Even more intangible is the reasoning behind the rhythm of cutting between actors in many of the one-on-one scenes, especially between Mads Mikkelsen and Hugh Dancy. The editors on the show agree that it is an instinctual decision.

"There are no rules, no set method," Wilkinson says.

"I find that the rhythm of the scenes between Will and Hannibal are largely dictated by performance. Mads and Hugh will give us pauses, looks, and beats and we have the option of expanding, contracting or leaving the pace as is. I would add, we are fortunate to have such an amazing cast, there is always so much good material to choose from."

There are always lines that the editors know have to be on camera, but good actors are always listening to each other's performances.

"Hugh Dancy and Mads Mikkelsen are two of the best," Doherty says. "Reaction shots can say volumes about what a scene is really about. Pay attention to when Will and Hannibal aren't speaking. It's terrific."

Philipson searches for the hidden story behind the words uttered. "The actors do a great job revealing the characters' complex motivations and rich emotions with very subtle looks, and we tend to hold on shots for a beat before or after a line read to allow those emotional beats to register."

The role of music is integral to the end viewing experience, but what about during the editing process?

"The episodes are scored after we've locked our episodes," says Philipson. "And we don't often work with Brian Reitzell before we've finished editing. However, we do put together a temporary score using music from previous episodes to help us find the right mood, tone and pace."

"The food montages are a signature of the show," Wilkinson says. "For those, we will request a classical cue from Brian so we can cut to the piece of music."

In the end, Philipson says that the final viewing experience can hold surprise even for those who have worked on cutting the episode together.

"It's always exciting to hear the soundtrack for the first time on the sound mixing stage, because Brian's music brings another level of energy and emotion to the show, and ties everything together with themes and colours specific to each episode."

MUSIC AND SOUND DESIGN

As the final stop on the trip to a completed episode, much rests on the shoulders of musician Brian Reitzell. But for such a heavy responsibility, Reitzell approaches it with as little forethought as possible.

"I don't start until I can sit down and work on it," he says. "I don't want to think about it. I just wait until I get a cut and then I start working on it. I don't read scripts, though. I find that it makes me overthink things a bit."

Reitzell will have discussions with Fuller about ideas that both might have for the coming season and how it might be incorporated, but the final implementation is, again, more instinctual.

"I'm not sure what episode they'll be in so I'll just be prepared and do it when it comes to me."

Other than on-camera music cures, such as Hannibal playing an instrument or attending a concert which are worked out in advance, everything else "has to come straight from the gut."

"Because it's horror, it's best for me to be shocked a bit for me to get that first response. That's so much of what the show is. And I think if you do it that way then you don't have to be so blatant about it. I think the music can cover whatever area where you might put a big, shocking car-falling-out-of-the-sky sound. You can do that in a way that stays with the audience more if you don't over-stylize it."

Mood informs his decisions as much as it does for the editors.

"For me, it's all mood. It's a mood piece all the way through. And it's a heightened reality and because of that there's constant mood sounds, mood music if you will, the whole time. The whole show is an opera."

Other less operatic influences for Reitzell are composers who favour less instrumentation instead of more.

"I really like scores that are quite minimal," he says. "And I've never liked TV music...it's manipulative and dumb. People are kissing and there are violins...

The food scenes in Hannibal often go hand-in-hand with classical music. The food itself, created by stylist Janice Poon [pictured below right] pairs exquisitely, both in look and content, with the music and mood of the show, like a steak paired with a rich, full-bodied cabernet sauvignon. [Below] Composer and Music Supervisor Brian Reitzell. Photograph by David Slade.

it's always so on-the-nose. With *Hannibal*, it demands there be a lot of music. So I find if I can use music in a way that feels more naturalistic then I can get away with it better. Having music that enters the way a car passing in the background would enter, or a bird chirping, or water dripping, or the air conditioner turning on...in some sort of very natural, ambient kind of way, and then I can get away with more."

A specific influence of this type of composition is the Japanese musician Tôru Takemitsu, whose minimalist work is thought of as a perfect fit with nature.

"I think that's what film music has to do so much of the time," Reitzell says. "It has to not be noticed, it has to be felt. And how do you do that in a way that feels like it isn't manipulating you?"

The roller-coaster ride that is *Hannibal* does require the occasional bombastic fanfare and Reitzell looks to the music used in *The Shining* for inspiration. Specifically in the first season, Reitzell drew from Stanley Kubrick's use of the heartbeat.

"And the first time I was working on the show, the sound effects people had put a heartbeat in there and I hated it because it felt so cliché."

But instead of abandoning the idea, he created his own in homage to the great filmmaker's scariest film.

"It was a real heart and it's moving a bit," he recalls. "I added some other tricks to it so it's not just a heart."

He also drew on the music chosen by Kubrick, particularly that of Polish composer Krzysztof Penderecki.

"The tone clusters, the string clusters, I love that stuff. I think Takemitsu did it even better than Penderecki, or used the orchestra in a more interesting way for me. Pendercki's stuff is bold, I absolutely love it."

Penderecki refused Kubrick's request to score the film, so the director instead used many of the composer's suggestions of existing music, eschewing the bulk of the score written by Wendy Carlos in the process.

"Some of the best musical moments in that movie were not made for the film," Reitzell says. "The stuff that was used was cool because it uses analog synthesis, these Moog synthesizers, with the orchestra...and that score is timeless and yet it uses electronics."

Perhaps there is no finer inspiration for the score of *Hannibal*, a show that exists outside of a specific time while still feeling relevant.

But the biggest stimulus for Reitzell's work on the show is the movement known as *musique concrete*. Developed by Pierre Schaeffer and associates in 1940s France at Studio d'Essai, it is a style of electroacoustic music that relies on the melding of natural sounds and music into a montage of sound.

Reitzell explains Phillips Records produced a series of records in France called 'Prospective 21e Siècle' that not only featured many avant garde compositions in the *musique concrete* style, some of which were made for television.

He also reports that Pierre Schaeffer received much of his money to record from French TV studios.

"So the fact that the stuff I'm doing with *Hannibal* [has] maybe its closest cousin in that kind of music. I find that completely natural."

[Above] Michael Rymer, director of seven episodes, on set for (left to right), season one, episode two "Amuse-Bouche"; season one, episode seven "Sorbet"; and season two, episode twelve "Tome-wan".

[Above] Peter Medak, director of two episodes including 'Hassun' season two, episode three, where Freddie Lounds (Lara Jean Chorostecki) has her day in court.

DIGESTIF
AUTHOR ACKNOWLEDGMENTS

Television is a hectic business and I would like to thank everyone who carved out space in their tightly-packed schedules to speak with me about their artistry and contributions to *Hannibal*.

First, a very special thanks to Bryan Fuller who was always passionate in his remarks and generous with his time. Huge thanks also to Loretta Ramos who kept the whole process moving and for her unwavering enthusiasm. Without her, this book would still be blank pages!

Special thanks go to the wonderful Mads Mikkelsen, Hugh Dancy, Laurence Fishburne, Caroline Dhavernas, and David Slade, who provided a unique perspective and fascinating insight on creating and populating Hannibal's new world.

Thank you to Danny Fredericks for arranging the time for these discussions. I am also grateful to François Dagenais for his insights into the creation of the amazing prosthetics work on *Hannibal*, and to Jenn Pattinson at Mindwarp Productions. Also, the incredibly talented Janice Poon was a cheerful and priceless resource.

There are so many more people to thank for making this book come alive, especially Martha De Laurentiis, Anthony Patterson, Ben Wilkinson, Brian Reitzell, Jason Klorfein, Christopher Hargadon, Angela Carbonetti, James Hawkinson, José Andrés, Anne Dolce, Gregory Haynes, Louise Caroline Castenskiold, Richard Lister, Matthew Davies, Michael Doherty, Patti Podesta, Robert Crowther, Steve Philipson, and Kirsti Tichenor and Travis Rutherford at Evolution. At NBC Universal, I would like to thank Cindy Chang, Liz Umeda, Joni Camacho, Rhion Magee, and Len Fogge and at Gaumont, Tim Farish, Robert Sorkin, Anne Bartnett and Ebony Sullivan.

Thanks also to my editor Beth Lewis and the staff at Titan for creating such a stunning book.

Finally, thank you to Fannibals everywhere. Without you this book and the show it celebrates would not be possible.